The Unhurried Chase
That Ended at L'Abri

The Unhurried Chase

". . . down the nights and down the days

BETTY CARLSON

That Ended at L'Abri

I fled Him down the arches of the years"

GOOD NEWS PUBLISHERS

Westchester, Illinois

Cover Photo: A. Kunz; Villars, Switzerland

Library of Congress Catalog Card Number 83-62688

ISBN 0-89107-304-3

Printing history
Tyndale House edition: Four printings 1970-1973
First Good News Publishers edition: 1984
Printed in the United States of America

To Lillabet
and her brothers and sisters

Contents

PART THREE: FOUND IN SWITZERLAND

"I fled Him, down the nights and down the days;
  I fled Him down the arches of the years;
I fled Him down the labyrinthine ways
  Of my own mind; and in the mist of tears
I hid from Him, and under running laughter.
  Up vistaed hopes I sped;
  And shot, precipitated,
Adown Titanic glooms of chasmed fears,
From those strong Feet that followed, followed after.
  But with unhurrying chase,
  And unperturbed pace,
Deliberate speed, majestic instancy,
  They beat — and a Voice beat
  More instant than the Feet —
'All things betray thee, who betrayest Me.' "

From the poem,
Hound of Heaven
by Francis Thompson
(Permission granted from
  Random House to quote this
  portion of the poem)

Foreword

W hen Betty and Gea visited us in Champéry, neither they nor
we realized it was a forerunner to L'Abri nor a forerunner
to anything. Neither did we know it was a preparation for Betty's
becoming a part of the community of L'Abri Fellowship, and at the
same time a preparation for us to open our home to not just two or
three people, but streams of people in the years to follow! The ac-
count of Betty Carlson's life preceding and during her visit to
Champéry gives an inkling of the many, many stories which others
could tell who have spent long hours in discussion and study in the
Swiss Alps and who have also found Christianity to be true.

Through many years now, Betty's life has been woven into the
lives of our family, even as our lives have into hers. She is not a
"L'Abri worker," but a writer who lives in the chalet God so clearly
chose for her in our midst — and she is a member of the little in-
ternational church as well as a part of the community. She shares
her chalet with L'Abri and also has a L'Abri member, Jane Stuart
Smith, living with her. Often she helps prepare the several festive
meals served each week to L'Abri guests and students in the Chesalet dining room.

If it had not been for Betty, the book *L'Abri* would never have
been written. One day she became convinced that God was asking
her to use a whole month's check "to send Edith off to write the
story of L'Abri." It was a scary thing for her to do, but feeling sure
it was right, she did it. She wrote out a check for the full amount,
praying that in "some way" her own expenses would be met. The

way God met her need is another story — but the fact is, He did. Her letter strongly urging me to go away for a month to write, and the combination of other circumstances making it possible to go, made it clear that that was exactly what I was meant to do. Betty kept encouraging me through that month with notes and 'phone conversations and assured me that the manuscript was "just great, Edith, keep it up," or I never would have had the courage to keep on.

Quietly in the background, Betty does things like this over and over again in her life. When she is convinced that a thing is important and that which God would have her do, she doesn't stop and protect herself from possible "loss" in the area of future security. For some years after I had written my book, it stayed under the bed in a suitcase, unpublished. Now I know that God wanted it to wait five years for chapter twenty-one, and also that He was waiting for my husband, Fran, to write *Escape From Reason* and *The God Who Is There*. It was all meant to come together in God's plan for the use of these books in people's lives. But Betty couldn't have known all this — on the surface it looked like a waste of money. But not once did she even *look* anything but sympathetic and understanding and pleased, as if writing books to *not* be published was the most wonderful and useful expenditure of money. Calmly she assured me, "It will be published at the right time."

Now I am sure this book of hers, *The Unhurried Chase That Ended at L'Abri,* written some years ago, but revised and brought up to date now, has also been waiting for just the right time to fit into the whole story of what God has been doing, and is doing, in the Swiss Alps. It gives you a glimpse into two lives, Betty's and Gea's, with very honest and realistic vividness. It may also give you some idea that there are hundreds, even thousands by now, of unwritten, true stories of how God brings those who are seeking Him into a place where they can hear *about* Him, and hear *Him,* know *about* Him, and know *Him.*

And when they come to know Him? There are changes in the individuals, but *not* a squashing out of personality, not a machine-mold called "Christian." Personality remains diverse. Betty's writing, her sense of humor, come out in this book to demonstrate clearly the diversity of the individual personalities of God's children, diverse personalities which go on being diverse for eternity!

What a fantastic future is ahead — an eternity of communication with the Personal God, and with all the diverse personalities in the total family of God. The reading ahead of you is your introduction to Betty Carlson!

— EDITH SCHAEFFER

Introduction
to the Introduction

An autobiography usually reveals nothing bad about its writer except his memory," said Franklin J. Jones. According to this standard, I qualify as an autobiographer. I can't remember what I had for lunch yesterday, the number of my license plates, nor my age (which proves that having a poor memory is not totally bad).

Had I known years ago that I was going to write this book, I would have taken notes or stamped on my letters: "Save for future publication."

When I was ten, I did start a diary. It said on page one: "Dear Dairy, It snowed yesterday, maybe we'll get snowed in and they'll have to close school. Cousin Eleanor gave me this dairy for Christmus. Also I got skates, sox, 5 dollers, 3 books, boxing gloves and a flashlight. Guess I'll go to bed, now I can read all night. P.S. Help me to lern to box good, God, so I can knock out them brothers of mine."

I could find nothing else in the "dairy" nor anyplace, but if I cannot remember details, I can always ask my younger brother. Ed is the one in our family with a strong memory. He knows the batting average of Stan Hack in 1935, how much a chicken dinner cost at Bishop's twenty years ago, and the fact that I never did knock him out.

BETTY CARLSON
HUEOMZ, SWITZERLAND

Introduction

People are always asking, "What do you do?"

You have heard them, and you have asked it yourself many times. At the supermarket, on a train, walking out of church, at PTA, eventually the question is asked, "What do you do?"

It is fine if you are a housewife, a plumber, or an anthropologist. You simply say, "I'm a housewife," or, "Plumbing is my line," or, "Dr. Aardvark, I'm connected with the Institute."

Nothing to it.

If you have taught for twenty-two years in the Wilson High School, you say easily, "I teach over at Wilson." And everybody is happy.

People love to know what other people do, and once you tell them, all is well.

I imagine if you are a fan dancer, you reply, "I'm a fan dancer," or possibly, "I dance with fans," though I am not positive, never having had the opportunity to ask.

"What do you do?" is an easy and pleasant question for most people. But then, there are a few, like myself, who would give anything to keep the conversation from turning to, "And what do *you* do?"

Perhaps you are wondering what I *do* do.

That's the point. I don't do anything. Anything orderly, that is, involving five days a week, eight hours a day, salary, fringe benefits, coffee breaks, picnic and banquet once a year, and pension. When asked what I do, I have only two monstrous choices: to tell the story of my life or pitifully answer, "I don't do anything."

17

Because it makes people unhappy, particularly Americans, I have learned to tone down Answer Number Two. In Europe it is all right to do nothing. They smile and assume you are an artist, a saint, or an existentialist. But we Americans, we want everybody to be doing something remunerative every minute, and it makes us genuinely uncomfortable to meet someone who doesn't do anything. Anything that is paying off right now.

I do not enjoy making others uncomfortable, so I end up telling the story of my life. Not that it is wildly exciting nor important, but it helps to explain that doing nothing, for some of us, can be quite exhausting. It does get involved, though, talking about yourself. Like yesterday, on the Greyhound bus, I was sitting next to a pleasant-faced, inquiring sort of lady. We exchanged the usual openers:

She said,

"Nice to sit up in front on one of these buses."

I nodded.

"I enjoy seeing where I'm going, don't you?"

I nodded again, pleasantly.

"What a day!"

"Lovely day," I replied.

There was a short silence as the bus driver counted the passengers, and immediately afterwards the question burst upon me, "What do you do?"

An actress friend once suggested,

"Why don't you make up something, if it bothers you so? Say you're a — spot remover in a cleaning establishment or a . . ."

But I'm too dumb. There isn't an acting bone in me, so I blunder in (now we're back on the bus),

"Why, I, ah . . . er, sort of go to school, and then I do a little writing."

The lady, dismissing the school part with a frown — she could plainly see I am past twenty-one and have no business going to school — retorted,

"Oh, you write? how interesting! For the *Saturday Post* or *McCall's* or . . . ?"

"Not exactly," I tried to explain, "I write a little column in a newspaper."

She seemed neither impressed nor satisfied; so I thought it would make her feel better if she knew I was a teacher. This generally makes people feel better, so modestly I said,

"I used to teach school."

"What do you mean, used to?" she sniffed.

Now I was trapped the other way. Even though I have my tired days, still I don't look quite as if I deserve retirement yet. Finally, with a deep sigh, I gave in and told my story, and it goes something like this. . . .

PART ONE

Going to Switzerland

CHAPTER I

Some Retire Sooner
Than Others

Y ou wished to see me, Miss Carlson?" The principal looked up as I walked into his office. He indicated that I was to sit in the chair in front of his desk.

"And what can I do for you?" He smiled faintly. And when he said, "I am always happy when my new teachers request to see me. It makes me feel as if they have confidence in me," he increased his smile.

I smiled back, weakly.

"I guess you won't be happy about seeing me, sir."

His smile froze, and he looked exactly like a principal; and I wished passionately I had done what I had considered doing, write him a letter *after* I had left town. But here I was. There he was. And that was the way it was.

I hastened to add,

"I haven't done anything wrong, Mr. Stone, and I do have confidence in you, and all that, but the point is . . ."

I gulped and looked out the window, nibbled on my last good fingernail, sighed deeply, and blurted out,

"Oh, I might as well just say it. I have decided to retire."

"You're going to *what,* Miss Carlson?" He coughingly laughed, "My dear, you've only been with us three months!"

Then rather shrilly, for a principal, "I've never *heard* of anyone retiring at the end of a couple of months." A little lower and softer, he added, "I really believe you better think it over for a few weeks, Miss ah . . ."

"Carlson," I supplied.

I was rattled, too, but I did remember my name.

"Yes, Miss Carlson, you think it over for a while," he said pleasantly and as if that were the end of the matter, "and then we'll talk about it again."

He started to fumble with some papers on his desk, but I wasn't through. I shook my head vigorously. It was now or never. I wasn't good at explaining, I never have been, but I had gone this far and I wasn't going to retreat.

"I have thought it over, very carefully, believe me," I said shakily, ignoring the fact that I had been dismissed. "I realize this sounds odd to you — to everybody, but, Mr. Stone, to be frank, I feel like I'm in a rut."

I scarcely knew what I was saying, but it came out with passion,

"I got such a smothered sensation the other day when I walked into the gym office, threw my keys down on the desk, picked up the clip board from the wall, put the whistle around my neck, bent over and scooped up a few volley balls . . ."

Mr. Stone wasn't looking at me. He was concentrating on something out the window, but I could tell by the way he was tapping his pencil, he was with me word for word.

I plowed on.

"All of a sudden I thought, 'And so here I'll be, twenty-five years from now, walking into the office, throwing my keys on the desk, picking up the clip board, putting on the whistle, scooping up balls, and all the time there are marvelously exciting things to do in life, and I should spend my life *blowing a whistle!*' "

Mr. Stone choked on something and had a violent coughing spell. He streaked toward the outer office for a drink of water. When he returned, he was still noisily clearing his throat. In his hand he had some papers which he had taken from the files. He sat down at his desk and began to shuffle through the papers.

"Ah yes," he said, still coughing a bit, "here it is."

Here is what, I thought anxiously.

"Yes, your application blank. I remember now." He gave me a knowing look. "I was, to express it mildly, impressed with it when I glanced through it last summer. In fact, I had never seen anything like it."

24

A suggestion of a grin brightened his face.

"To say the least, *the very least*," he said, "your interests are broad, Miss Carlson."

He flipped a page, studied it, and for a moment I thought that coughing spell was going to overtake him, but he rallied and was able to say huskily,

"Under hobbies, you have listed: 'Flying, playing the oboe, most sports (except ski jumping and ice hockey), cartooning and pastel painting, fixing up old cars, hiking, traveling (Switzerland, I hope), boating, poetry, classical music, writing, astronomy, psychology, reading, designing . . .'"

He paused, looked directly at me as if he were seeing me for the first time, and said slowly and pointedly,

"Are you really interested in *all* these things?"

I slumped lower in the chair and nodded pathetically. He shook his head and slumped down in his chair.

I couldn't think of a thing to say.

It seemed as if I should defend myself, but when he read the list it sounded foolish, even to me. He turned and looked out the window again. He kept staring out the window, and I sat thinking, I wish I didn't always upset people. I didn't really mean to.

Finally Mr. Stone swung around and looked my way again, but he didn't look like a principal. There was something different about his eyes.

"I think I agree with you," he said pleasantly. "Anybody with *your* interests shouldn't, ah . . . spend the next twenty years blowing a whistle!" His eyes twinkled nicely. "In fact, I wonder how you've had time to teach these three months?"

"To tell the truth, Mr. Stone, it hasn't been easy."

He put his head back and laughed, and then I laughed, mostly because he was laughing. He removed his glasses, wiped his face with his hand, and said, almost to himself,

"It's easy to bog down earning a living. It isn't this job, or any job, that makes a man dull. We're the ones who become dull."

I broke in, "I agree with you."

I blushed and started over. "I don't mean you're dull, Mr. Stone, but I'm thinking of myself and this job. If I thought teaching was for me, I know it could be a good life, but I'm not a teacher. I don't know enough to teach. I only majored in physical education because I like to play tennis and swim."

The principal and his young teacher, now retiring, said more and probably less.

As I was leaving the office, Mr. Stone asked, "Why are you interested in Switzerland?"

"I don't know exactly, just know I'm going there someday."

He smiled and nodded, "I'll be looking for a postcard."

CHAPTER II

When in Doubt

S witzerland proved to be later. In the meantime, I exercised a theory of mine — when in doubt, go to school. I had not worked my way through college, in fact, I had never earned any money until I taught the last three months. So when I went "into retirement," I thought it best not to suggest to my father that he support me, that is, if I could possibly avoid it.

My father liked people who finished what they started, and oddly enough, I do too, but I had no words at the time to explain that I was not really quitting, I was beginning. To prove to my father how determined I was to be self-supporting, I applied for a scholarship *and* a job.

To my parents I announced the new venture with enthusiasm. There was never any holding me back, once my mind was made up. From the moment I decided to change direction, right or wrong, sensible or foolish, I would talk about the new cause with such fervor that I not only convinced the people involved that I was launching into a noble and worthwhile enterprise, but also myself. By the time I had finished explaining my latest project, I felt like the captain I had recently seen in an advertisement. He is standing with one foot resting on the globe of the world, and his expression is that of adventure and conquest. If I remember correctly, the captain is advertising chewing tobacco. . . .

Well, perhaps my parents were not *quite* as enthusiastic as I was. My father said nothing, and my mother reminded me (gently) of the one or two times I had collapsed in college from overdoing. I remembered well what my doctor had told me,

"There is no reason why you cannot live a reasonably normal life, if . . ."

"But who wants to live *a reasonably normal life*," I had blurted out.

He said kindly, having an artistic daughter of his own, "It isn't so bad being reasonably normal!"

We had talked about what I was doing, and I had had to admit that I was following a program which included everything I wasn't supposed to do, and quite a bit more. His parting advice was, "Don't take on so much. You don't have to do everything before you're twenty!"

To those of us over forty, the routine the doctor outlined is appealing — go to bed early, live a nice, unhurried life, avoid stimulants, and do one thing at a time.

But to me, in my late teens and in love with living, it was a death sentence. I knew the doctor was right, though, and for almost a month, I followed his regime and it worked wonderfully; but soon I was going at my pace again, only to learn, over and over, that the doctor knew what he was talking about.

This helps to explain why my parents did not pressure me too much about giving up teaching. I wasn't "only teaching." It was getting increasingly difficult to find time for my flying lessons, the different orchestras I was playing in, the scout troop I directed, a full social life, plus frequent trips to Chicago to visit friends. My parents knew I would not last, and they also knew the scholarship and job were not the right answer. But I left for Chicago in high spirits, mentally with my foot "resting on the globe of the world."

The ad I answered sounded excellent:

"Girl wanted to help mother with three children. Private bedroom and time for studying."

I knew nothing about taking care of children nor helping a mother, but the private room and time for studying won me.

When I was studying in my private room the second night, Mr. Murphy knocked on my private door.

"You don't mind," he said pleasantly, "if we move the baby in here for the night, do you?"

Before I could mind, in came the crib and baby.

He explained, "My wife has been a little upset since she came home from the hospital. The baby's breathing seems to bother her at night, but I don't imagine you'll even notice it."

Not even notice it! !

28

After the infant had been with me four or five seconds, I understood why the mother was a "little" upset. It was both fascinating and alarming: fascinating that one tiny baby could make *that* much noise, and alarming to think that each rattling intake of air might be the child's last gasp.

When I staggered out to fix breakfast at six the next morning, I was in worse shape than the mother, but the baby was cooing sweetly, looking rested and fit.

I was crestfallen. I honestly wanted to succeed at the job, but I didn't need a gypsy to read the tea leaves in the bottom of my cup to tell me that this was not the environment for a person who is supposed to avoid stimulants. Even to this day if I have a reason for wanting to stay awake, I try to recall what the baby sounded like, and who took my place, and how long they lasted.

CHAPTER III

A Game Called Squash

S wallowing pride is harder for some than others, but it was either choke on it or let it choke me. I chose the former, gave up the private room and baby, and called home. My parents were great. Not one hint of "I told you so." They appeared nearly as surprised as I was that it did not work out. They listened with sympathy (long distance, collect) while I told in detail about the wheezing infant and the upset mother and the struggling student in Chicago without a room and job. At their suggestion I moved in with a good friend on the South Side, which was what I really wanted to do in the first place, and my father said he would have a check in the mail that afternoon in case I was low.

My friend was the assistant recreational director, women's division, of the Hyde Park YMCA, and our underfurnished, overheated apartment on East Fifty-third Street, a few blocks away, soon became an extra club room for the Y, both M and W. In a short while, we gathered in another roommate who had majored in home economics. With an expert cook among us, it wasn't long before Dale, who lived above us, became a regular boarder; then there was Joe, the bellhop, working his way through the University of Chicago, and his friends, who stopped quite regularly just before mealtime.

Switzerland was out of the question, because of the war. By the autumn of 1941 I was ready to go to work again, and so when I was offered a position at the Woman's Athletic Club of Chicago, I gladly accepted. It was not a whistle-blowing job. I was to give private lessons in swimming, diving, badminton, and squash.

It was because of the squash that I was able to beat out a couple of strong contenders for the position. They did not know how to play squash; well, I didn't either, but my friends at the Y told me to put on the application blank that I was a squash enthusiast. "You will be," they insisted, "after Pete gets through with you."

Pete was the champion of the Y; and it was true — by the time he was through with me, I was aware that squash is more than a vegetable. And so I got the job, because I could play squash, but as it turned out, the ladies of the Woman's Athletic Club were not squash minded.

Try as hard as I did, I was able to interest only one member in squash during my year there. And not only were the ladies not squash minded, they rarely used the lovely pink-tiled swimming pool. I never did learn why it was called the Athletic Club. I doubt that some of the members even knew there were badminton courts, exercising rooms, a squash court, and a swimming pool; and so, after a year, the lovely position went out of existence, because the only two people who consistently used the recreational facilities were Ottilia and I.

Ottilia was the Swedish maid in charge of the locker room. She would stand guard while I had my swim, and I would watch her while she had her daily workout. "In Sweden, we are used to physical activity," she said, as she moved her short, stout body through the water. I never knew how old she was (at least sixty), but she had the agility of a young person.

We spent hours together in the office by the side of the swimming pool waiting for an occasional member to appear. The days never dragged with Ottilia around. She was exceptionally interesting and well read. By training and heart, she was a teacher, but when an older brother sent her a ticket for Chicago, she left her teaching position in Gothenborg. Because of financial trouble she was never able to secure a teaching certificate in this country, but she never lost her love for the profession, and her love for reading, for learning. During our year together she poured into my hungry mind the best she knew.

We read and discussed three or four books a week, and among other things she taught me how to embroider and to bake. Several mornings around Christmas, I got up at 4:30 to set dough — large pans of dumpy, damp dough. My roommates never got over my rising before dawn to make them homemade bread, but I wanted to bring samples to Ottilia to see if I was really getting Swedish rye. One morning she tasted a piece with our ten o'clock coffee and nodded,

"Ja, yust fine."

Ottilia underlined for me how much more important it is *what* we are in life, not *who*. I often wondered at the strangeness of the situation; this mature, wise woman picking up towels and emptying ashtrays for ladies who knew her only as the locker-room maid.

I failed in one respect with Ottilia. I never could interest her in squash. "What foolishness," she frowned, "running between two walls swinging at a little ball. It is better to hoe a garden. You get the same exercise and have beans and yuicy tomatoes for your table!"

CHAPTER IV

Detour

The restful, stimulating year at the Woman's Athletic Club left its mark. For the first time I wanted to go to school to learn, not to fill in time, not for fun, but to find strong answers to the questions I was accumulating. I headed west, definitely the long way to Switzerland, but the war was blazing all around Switzerland, and the small, peaceful country seemed farther away than ever.

The reason for going to Oregon was simple. A good friend wrote that Oregon State was a fine school, and she had picked a place for me to live in the shadow of a mountain. Mary's Peak is a small mountain, a foothill, but to me from the Middle West, seeing my first mountain, it was a wonderful mountain. I loved walking toward it, never reaching it, only moving toward it. The squash racquet grew dusty. It did seem foolish to run around in a small, enclosed room swinging at a ball when there were mountain trails to explore, books to open, questions to ask.

Above all, I learned to question in the foothills of Oregon. I had a sort of innocence, actually it was more ignorance than innocence; but it is common among young people brought up in happy, adjusted home situations where you have no reason to doubt, mistrust, or even hate those with whom you are in daily contact. I assumed people in authority were trustworthy, particularly teachers and professors with their rich background of study and training. Then came books; for me, books were the final authority. If it was printed in a book, I believed it; but this became impossible, wild, chaotic, as I began to open and shut a thousand books. Then in Oregon a beloved professor said, "Just because you read something in a book, you must not assume it is truth."

This opened up a new direction for me, and overnight I began to question everything. I was like a mouse in an old house who sits down on the pendulum of the grandfather clock when it is at its farthest point to the right and with one movement finds itself at the opposite point. Questioning everything became the ruling force in my life.

I looked up a copy of Tom Paine's *Age of Reason.* As a student in high school I read it with shock, because it cut across everything I had been taught at home and in the Lutheran church. But in Oregon, propped up against a tree in the shade of Mary's Peak, I read the book with delight. Scornfully, I thought, how naïve can you be? Blind trust in a church and a system of belief is ignorance. My parents are Lutherans because their parents were Lutherans, and so should I be a Lutheran? *Stupid,* I told my mountain. I'm not going to believe because somebody else believes. I will believe because I believe, and I choose this day not to believe. I give you back, mountain, my inherited faith. Hide it in your bowels along with my other childhood ghosts. You can have them all — Santa Claus, elves, fairies, Matthew, Mark, Luke — I'm moving into the *real* world where I can use my head for thinking and questioning and learning.

I told only the mountain that I was finished with believing. It was always painful for me to upset those whom I cared for; so I guarded my secret well, but this was not difficult. We Scandinavians are reticent by nature; and having four grandparents from Sweden, that is a lot of Swedish blood in American veins. We Nordics do not readily discuss our religious convictions, nor do we easily communicate our inner distresses.

Perhaps this helps to explain the reputation Scandinavians have for being cheerful and carefree. Their grief is not worn on their sleeves. When they cry, they cry inside. When desperate, they bury it deep; and when they search for reality, they search silently. From the moment I gave up the faith of my fathers, I started stretching hungrily for answers to the questions that began to tumble about in my unquiet mind.

Having unshackled myself from religious and family restrictions, I felt free, deliciously free, but for such a short time. The lilting liberty, the sense of joyous freedom, was over almost as it began. Without my being truly aware of what was happening, my freedom rapidly became a grievous and tragic burden. I could ques-

34

tion, yes, and I did question and question and question, but the questioning only led to more questions. And the more I asked, Where is God? Who is God? Is there a God? What is truth? Is there truth? Does it matter? Who am I? Why am I? Where am I going? — the more I questioned, the more confused and dissatisfied I became. There were answers, all right, answers on all sides; but none satisfied, other questions gushed over them, like water over a poorly constructed dam.

But having an unquiet mind and a lost faith does not completely alter the same old you, and I found the USO the right place to forget how lost I really was. The friend who had interested me in coming to Oregon was the director of the USO. Within a few days after my arrival in Corvallis, I was signed up as a volunteer.

One of the ways I helped was to assist in the art class. I was little help to the teacher, because I could only paint mountains; but we finally located one soldier who also liked mountains. And so every Tuesday night, Ted and I would talk and paint mountains.

He had recently returned to the States from the North African invasion; and one evening he mentioned casually something about a friend of his who was a Red Cross worker. He wondered if I might know her, as she had gone to Oregon State.

"Her?" I exclaimed. "Do you mean the Red Cross sends women overseas?"

"Oh, sure, women are all over these days."

I had to restrain myself from writing the Red Cross headquarters that night to see if they needed a recreational director in the vicinity of Switzerland; but having only a few months left to get a master's degree, I remembered that I liked to finish things (and so did my father who was supporting me) and I stuck it out.

Two days before I was scheduled for an interview with a Red Cross representative, I pounded out the last words of my thesis. I was beginning to feel the salt spray on my face, when, wouldn't you know, some overzealous, conscientious executive rechecked my health record and decided that I was a poor risk for overseas. "But we have a wonderful opening in Washington which we are sure you will enjoy," they told me cheerfully.

"No," I said, "thank you very much, but no, you see, I'm going to Switzerland, and. . . ." Hopefully I added, as an afterthought,

"If you should get hard up and have to take the poor risks, you will call me, won't you?"

The call from the Red Cross never came. They never got *that* desperate, so I went home to Rockford to wait and to sit and think.

One day when I was out doing errands, I walked into the downtown post office to mail a letter, and the "Join the Navy and see the world" poster caught my eye. Probably I have seen thousands of these signs in my life time, but that morning the "See the world" part turned on as if it were an exploding fireworks display. Having nothing else to do, I ran up the stairs to the recruiting office. Vaguely I had heard about the WAVES, and thought: it never hurts to get a little information.

For the benefit and protection of the curious, the greedy, and the ignorant, like myself, *don't ever* visit a recruiting office to ask a few questions — write, telephone, send a cable, but *never* innocently walk in!

Before I could say, "Anchors aweigh," they had counted my teeth, measured my height, and performed the other routine tasks connected with signing away one's life to the Navy. I was assigned to the unit leaving for the Naval Training Center in New York City at the end of the week. I suspect they run those recruiting officers through two or three charm schools, several Dale Carnegie courses, and the 1943 counterpart of Slenderella and Vic Tanny's. The curious part is that in a tour of duty that took me from New York to Hawaii and back again, never again did I encounter the same hospitality as in that recruiting office; nor do I think Dale Carnegie would have been at all happy with some of the language that was snarled at us seawomen as we were cut loose from our slovenly civilian attitudes; but it was a riotous, sobering, and unforgettable two years, and most surprising of all, it did get me to Switzerland after I was honorably discharged.

Join the Navy and
See the... Navy

Y ou've *what?*" my father roared.

I didn't know how to announce my latest project. When I walked into the recruiting office, I had no notion of joining the Navy; in fact, I disliked women in uniform. It seemed undignified, and so I couldn't think how to tell my family that even though I looked the same as I had seven hours before, I was not the same. Seated at the table with them was a WAVE, a raw recruit in the women's division of the glorious United States Navy.

My sister gave me an opening. She said, "I saw Bill this morning; you know, he is the fellow who sat behind me in English until he left school last month to join the Army." She turned to me and said, "Will you please pass the butter?"

"Yes," I said, quite cheerfully, "the butter, yes, aha . . . , that reminds me, when I was out shopping this morning, I joined the Navy. . . ."

That's when my father exploded, "You've *what?*"

Talk about upsetting people. I had reached a new high. My father was furious. "I've never *known* anyone to rattle around in life quite the way *you* do! *Joined the Navy! !* . . . Why I . . ." and so forth, and so on. It was curious about my father. He was a kind man, one could even say, mild, but he had an explosive streak, like me (or I guess, I was like him), and we differed radically on one point. He had to get used to a new idea before he warmed up to it. I loved to plunge into something, and then get used to it.

So, what a relief! Now that he knew I was in the Navy, we

could talk calmly about other things, like, how I was able to pass the physical. "Well," I explained, "if you enlist, you don't have to be quite as healthy as an officer, and," I added slyly, "you don't have to tell everything you know."

"You're not going to be an officer?" my sister said, looking at me with about as much disapproval as my father, "after six years of college?"

These quiz programs finished me, but I rattled on, "I couldn't pass the eye examination. Officers have to see!"

My father said nothing, but he did exchange a knowing look with my mother. . . .

Camp Elliott, where I was shipped after I surprisingly survived the indoctrination course in New York City and later, the Yeoman School in Oklahoma, was located on a desert about twenty miles from San Diego. They stressed at Yeoman School the efficiency of the Navy, and that it would be a major offense to arrive at one's new station late.

I wasn't taking chances. I had my friends deposit me at the military bus depot in San Diego at 5:45 A.M. We had been up since 4:00. My military orders read:

"Report at 8 A.M."

I was there, all right, in fact, before 7:00, and I doubt if I can convey to you my astonishment to learn that it wouldn't have made any difference to anyone if I had arrived a few weeks or months late. The situation was so fouled up, I had difficulty locating an officer who might have a clue *what* to do with me. Afterwards I learned — and may I add, that was one of the maddening features of military life, always learning things *afterwards* — I learned *afterwards* that Camp Elliott was a Marine base, and the Navy was in the process of taking it over. After we all got acquainted, the sailors were jolly glad to have us highly trained WAVES help in the scullery, and to pick up cigarette butts with those long pointed sticks and to swab decks.

But the best fun on the desert was helping to build a recreational program. Four of us were given a clean bill of sale to do whatever we felt needed to be done to help "build morale." Believing in the power of the press I got myself assigned to the camp newspaper. There, through a column called "Sally Ho," we crusaded for our cause. By the time I left for Hawaii, Camp Elliott looked more like a country club than a naval station. There were two swimming pools, tennis courts, a golf course (mostly sand traps), bowling alleys, a library, and grass and trees planted around the chapel. I hated to leave, but when I learned WAVES were being sent overseas, I applied for Switzerland, and was promptly shipped to Hawaii.

CHAPTER VI

Overseas, But Wrong Sea

It seemed a shame — with so many intriguing places to visit in Hawaii and white beaches to enjoy — to spend the days in a naval office, so I got on a night shift. I believe it would have worked if everybody in our open quonset hut, and for six miles around, had been on the same schedule; but about the time we night workers were going to bed, everyone else was getting up. I did work in the sightseeing, the beach, and my job. The only thing missing was sleep; and this being one of the things my doctor told me I needed lots of, I landed in the naval hospital.

Celebrating New Year's Eve in a Navy hospital ward near Honolulu wasn't as restricting as you might think. A friend — who was Hawaiian, and assigned to the bed next to me — had her brother bring up a bottle of Scotch, and around midnight she set off a firecracker under my bed so I'd "never forget New Year's Eve in Hawaii!" And I never have.

I was in the hospital about one month, and a few days after I returned to active duty, I was mustered out of the Navy. The war was over, and the year of peace, 1946, had begun.

Within a few weeks, a few hundred of us were standing on the deck of a hospital ship waving good-bye to good friends in Hawaii. While we were saying our "alohas" and soft music was playing, a gruff voice with a Brooklyn accent called us down to the mess hall; and as we were eating, the ship left Pearl Harbor, rounded Diamond Head and put out to sea. We were disappointed not to be on deck, but I was so impressed with how smoothly the ship was moving, I commented once or twice, "There's hardly any motion."

We had flown over to Hawaii, so this was my first voyage on the sea. Shortly after we left the mess hall, we hit the ocean proper,

40

and as the small ship plowed into the giant waves, we headed for our triple-deck bunks. I shall spare you the details of the next six days and six nights, one hundred and forty-four hours, eight thousand and six hundred and forty minutes of seasickness. It was bad enough to be seasick, but I had a sickness of heart too. All my life I had waited for this moment when I would stand on the deck of a ship, salt spray in face and hair blowing back; and here I was, down under in the hold of the ship, and the thought of even raising my head, unbearable.

But I have a short memory. In a year I was on another ship, this time headed for Norway. I did somewhat better on the Atlantic; at least I got to the deck.

CHAPTER VII

By Way of Norway

I'm a veteran! Do you hear me? I'm a veteran!" I snapped on the light.

Laila ducked her head under the sheet and mumbled, "Fine, I hear you."

We had taken in a movie that night and had gone to bed about midnight. This was somewhat later. She added in the same calm voice, "Shall I call in the Navy band and we'll . . . ."

"Don't kid, my friend, I'm dead serious. It just hit me. I probably can study in Europe under the G.I. Bill. I'm a veteran!"

Laila was my roommate at the University of Washington. From the Navy I returned home for a few months, but I soon headed west again. A nice feature about military life, it relieves you of the pressure of thinking, so my mind had had two dormant years; but from the day of my discharge, the questions began to erupt again.

Laila did much to stir up my interest in the Scandinavian countries. It was her dream to earn enough money to be able to take her mother back to Norway, where she had been born. Switzerland was not forgotten, but my interest began to cover all of Europe. Laila had pictures, maps, and books, particularly on Norway and Sweden, and night after night we pored over them.

A plan began to take form in our minds and on paper. I would go with Laila and her mother to Norway first, and later we would go to Sweden to visit my relatives. Then we heard of a youth hostel project in southern France which was also going to include a bicycle tour in Switzerland. We talked, planned, wrote letters, dreamed, and that was as far as we went.

And then the night I am speaking about, we saw a Norwegian film on the life of Grieg. Grieg was a friend of Rikard Nordraak, the composer of the Norwegian national anthem. In one scene, the two musicians and friends were discussing the many things they wanted to do in life; and Grieg was gently teasing Nordraak, because he was in such haste to live. The story ended on the poignant note of the death of Rikard Nordraak two years after the young artists had met.

When my friends and I were walking back to our boarding house, back to our routine lives, back to our books, back to our planning, back to our talk, the words of Nordraak taunted me, "We mustn't wait, friend, dreams are to be lived *now*."

Suddenly and surely at two A.M., whatever day that was, I knew I couldn't wait another month, another year, to get my dream going; and in the middle of that night the idea came, my possible stepping-stone to Europe. As a veteran of the war (which I was), I was studying at the University of Washington under the G.I. Bill of Rights, but it had never lighted up in my cluttered mind that this program might include foreign countries.

The first thing after breakfast, I ran to the Veterans' office on campus. The personnel officer said calmly, "Certainly you can study in Europe under the G.I. Bill. Paris, Rome . . . ."

"Switzerland?" I asked hoarsely.

He reached in the file cabinet for some papers.

"I don't know much about Switzerland; most of our students go to France or . . . ." He studied the bulletin in front of him. "Here it mentions Switzerland, yes, Lausanne, Switzerland. Besides the university, there's a music conservatory and . . . ."

"Thank you," I said, as I was halfway out of the room. "Wonderful! I've heard everything I've wanted to hear. I'll be back in twenty minutes to fill out the forms, but first I have to make a phone call."

Even though I was free, independent, and past twenty-one, I liked keeping my family informed. Soon I was giving the exciting details to my mother, thankful she had answered the phone. My father had recently had a heart attack and I dreaded talking directly to him for fear I'd say the wrong thing and upset him. Suddenly I heard him say to my mother, "I want to talk to her too."

Something tightened inside me. I leaned against the wall and tried to calm down, at the same time marshaling my forces so I'd say the right things and not always have to upset him. I started to say something, but he said, "Wait, I want to tell you something first." I slumped down on the bench prepared for the worst. The agony of thinking I might have to defy my father crushed me; and so, when he first began speaking to me, I didn't really understand what he was saying. He was telling me how sobering it was to be close to death and how it causes a man to think. He felt God had given him extra time in his life, time to do things differently.

He said, "While you were in the Navy, and I was allowed to go back to my office part-time, I spent a couple of weeks rearranging my business affairs. I'll skip the details, but this is the part that will interest you. I wasn't going to tell you for a couple of years, but your call today convinces me the time is right." He took a deep breath and continued, "I have set up a trust fund for you." Quickly he added, "It's not a great amount, but the checks have been accumulating now for over a year, so it looks like, if you want to go to Switzerland, you're on your way!"

I couldn't find adequate words then, and I can't now. There are solemn, wonderful moments in life when words fail us; but I danced out of the phone booth, laughing, crying, and singing, and raced to tell Laila we were on our way to Europe. . . .

The traveling got under way with a roar. Enthusiasm and determination are contagious; and so, the day before Easter, 1947, Laila, her mother, and I were peering down from the deck of a Norwegian ship at a blur of faces turned up toward us in the harbor of Kristiansand, Norway; and within a few weeks, many of those faces became dear to us. I shall never quite get over the Norwegian people, their wonderful joy in living — and what hospitality! There is a ruggedness about Norway, and the Norwegians, which strongly appealed to me, a ruggedness tempered with beauty and gentleness.

Laila's cousin Astrid whisked us off on a skiing trip the day after we landed at Kristiansand. A bus took us back into the mountains, and when the bus couldn't go any farther, we loaded our luggage on a sleigh drawn by a horse. When the horse couldn't go any farther, we carried our own bags, and this included an accordian, boxes of canned food, and our personal belongings. First the path was fairly easy, then it got steeper and the snow deeper. It took us part of the night to get to our destination, a primitive cabin tucked back in the mountains. Laila and I had never been so tired and hungry and exhilarated in our lives, and would have liked to stay indefinitely in the mountain cabin. But Laila had cousins, aunts, and uncles from the southern coast of Norway to beyond the Arctic Circle, and we did not want to miss visiting one of them.

Late in May, we left Laila's mother with her sisters and ninety-year-old father on a small island which was as near to Russia as I've been, and headed for Sweden. In order to get to Narvik, where we were to get the train, one of Laila's uncles took us in his fishing boat. Here I fulfilled the desire to stand on deck with the salt spray in my face and my hair blowing back. The water was calm and the breeze gentle. Our small boat took us in and out of fjords and islands which only God and these fishermen ever see; and it was light all night long, because we were in the land of the midnight sun. All we did was look and wonder. The uncle sat at the control, steering the little vessel, smoking his pipe, and smiling.

Places on maps which previously had been small, meaningless dots began to be people — interesting people, kind people, likable people, people who had suffered terribly in the war and whose hearts reached ours in a way that gave significance to all that we did in Norway.

At Narvik we caught the train for Stockholm. Sweden enchanted us too. It had not experienced the destruction of war within its boundaries, so everything was tidier. We found the same hospitality as in Norway and were made to feel at home. So it went. Norway, Sweden, and Denmark in the spring and early summer. Then Laila rejoined her relatives in Kristiansand, and I flew to Paris to meet my hostel group.

My first glimpse of Paris was from the back of a bicycle. I arrived at night, and my bike came later. The following day a friend gave me a lift to the air terminal, so I could pick it up. Two adults on one bicycle has the element of adventure; but going across the Place de la Concorde in the midst of wild traffic — I, intoxicated with seeing with my own eyes landmarks familiar to all, and the one steering the bike pointing to the right, to the left, up and down — was life at its liveliest. The fact that a gendarme was waving his club at us and shouting, "Attention, imbéciles, attention!" only added to the charm.

Our hostel group worked for a month in the Pyrénées on the Spanish border. I mean worked. We carried enough rocks that summer to build a bridge across the Atlantic. To relax after the work project, we cycled for a month in southern France in temperatures ranging between 95 degrees and 115, the hottest, driest summer in forty years, or some such record. As we'd drag through the poor, dirty villages with every shutter closed, we always kept hoping that in the next village we'd fine a nice, clean drugstore with a fountain where they served ice cold cokes. We learned to be thankful for a small grocery store with warm sour wine. Finally we persuaded our leader to let us take a bus from Nice to Geneva.

What luxury! We piled the bikes on top and prepared to enjoy the trip. As we were crossing the Alps, somewhere between the two cities, our driver took the wrong road at a fork. As dusk and fog descended upon us, the road narrowed down to a mountain path barely wide enough for one car, let alone the possibility of meeting another. Our driver, as frightened and lost as his passengers, knew there was no possibility of going back, so kept going at a creeping pace. Suddenly, he shouted, "Mon Dieu, we are saved!" It was a small mountain inn. The owner could hardly believe that a bus had come up the narrow trail, and in fog.

It turned out to be a hilarious night. After a couple of friends of mine and I had had something warm to eat and drink, we opened our sleeping bags under a table and went to sleep. Several others in the group sang and drank most of the night.

As we approached Switzerland the next morning, I was alternately ill at ease and exhilarated. Now that it was so close, I began to fear I'd be disappointed. The bus driver let us off at the frontier, and as we pushed our bikes across the border, immediately the doubting was gone. The real Switzerland was even better than the picture in my mind which had been there, off and on, ever since I read *Heidi*. We stayed in Switzerland only a few days on this hosteling trip, but long enough for me to know I had found what I was looking for, and that I would be back.

From Switzerland we went to Paris again, and after a round of operas, museums, sightseeing, my friends went back to the States. I bought a good map of northern Europe, put some fresh air in the tires, and headed the bike toward Norway. I figured that as long as I could point, smile, and say, "Thank you," Belgium, Luxembourg, Holland and Germany would prove no different than southern Europe. This was true. It was a memorable trip, and within a month or so I was knocking at Tante Petra's door in Kristiansand, Norway, across the street from the birthplace of Rikard Nordraak.

In the autumn I returned home. It seemed enough for one year, and besides, I had started writing letters to my family urging them to make reservations for a trip to Europe in the following spring. I decided I better go home and see that they were doing this. Then, of course, if they insisted, I would be willing to accompany them.

CHAPTER VIII

The Night Maid

The idea came to us together. I was talking to my friend, Bernice. Our parents were in Florida for the winter, and we were saying how nice that must be. Why don't we go too? was the idea. After all, Bernice said, or maybe I did, somebody has to work in those hotels lining the beach. Why couldn't we? We rounded up another friend and headed for Miami by way of New Orleans and the Mardi Gras. I knew a couple of WAVES who lived in the Latin Quarter, and they had told me to come on down sometime.

It took a few days to get over the Mardi Gras, but in another week or so we were pulling into the driveway of the small hotel where our parents were staying. Quickly we assured our fathers we were not planning to stay with them.

"What are you doing here?" Bernice's father asked suspiciously.

"We're going to be night maids," we said together, feeling like characters in a musical comedy.

"Night maids!" our mothers exclaimed. They knew how deficient we were at bed-making and dusting. They thought the idea was extremely funny.

That made us so mad, we went directly to the beach to survey the hotels. Finally I saw a tall, new building that impressed me as a fine place to work.

"Let me out here," I said. "I like the looks of this one — think I'll give it a try."

We decided it was wiser to break up to get our jobs. Up until the moment I got out of the car, I had had courage to burn. It is interesting how brave you are when you are laughing and joking with others about doing something out of your line; but suddenly, here I was, in the linen room of the fabulous Sea View Hotel, and

48

I had just told the severe-looking housekeeper that I would like to be one of her night maids. My knees felt limp and shaky, like after a long horseback ride, and I didn't recognize my own voice.

She eyed me suspiciously. "Ever had any experience, miss?"

She was counting sheets when I came in, and after she had looked me over, she went back to her counting. I hastened to tell her how I had worked in my uncle's drugstore for a couple of weeks and how I had experience behind the fountain in the USO, and how I had worked for a whole summer at a "resort" making beds and waiting on tables (I was referring to a camp where I had been a counselor). I thought it best not to mention the teaching.

She gave me a pained look and continued counting. I could see she wasn't impressed. I stood there trying to look industrious and irresistible. Finally she thumped down the last five sheets and said wearily, "You're hardly what I had in mind, but I'm desperate. At least you look honest, and that's more than I can say for most of them who come in here, so I'm giving you a try."

She turned to a board behind her and removed a key.

"This is for your locker," she said. "Ask the bellboy out there to show you where to check out a uniform. Then come back, and you can go around with Martha tonight." Grimly she added, "You better pay attention, because tomorrow night you'll be on your own! We'll discuss your salary later. No point filling out a lot of papers if you don't last the week."

That first night when Martha, the experienced night maid, was taking me around and explaining things to me, she stopped in the middle of a corridor and put her arm around me (I must have looked so bewildered) and said kindly, "Now dearie, don't let the people scare you. It don't matter if we ain't had the education like them — you jest talk up to them like you knew something too." She laughed loudly, "I do it all the time, and they like it." Then she added seriously, "But not to Mrs. Carter; jest say, 'Yes'm, no'm,' she ain't much for smart talkin'." She patted me on the cheek, "You'll get along fine, don't worry. Be natural."

Martha was wonderful. A complete contrast to Mrs. Carter, the housekeeper. Martha taught me all she knew about being a night maid, plus passing on her colorful philosophy of life. I learned to turn down beds and give rooms a quick going over, so they would look fresh and cozy when the guests returned from the dog races, horse races, or night clubs. Patiently she worked with me on the studio couches. Each one was different, and the pillows had to go in special places. It was all most confusing.

"Don't get nervous," she said. "You'll catch on. Now, one other thing, don't ever clean the rooms. That's what the day maids do." She added confidentially, "I'd never be a day maid! There's jest no style to their job."

I don't know if I can explain it, but the first night I came on duty and slipped into my peach pastel uniform with the frilly white apron and neat headband, I felt I was in a play. The entire hotel was my stage. The joke was, I've never been in a play and know nothing about acting, but if ever I acted a part, it was there at the Sea View when I gave my all as a French night maid. Why I wasn't Swedish or Spanish, I'll never know. But, as if I had no control over it at all, when I met the first couple in the hall on my way to the first room I was to put in order, I tipped my head graciously and heard myself murmur, "Bonsoir, madame et monsieur!"

The gentleman bowed slightly in return, and the stunningly dressed lady said, "Good evening, my deah!"

As long as I live, I'll remember every moment of the first night, on my own, as a night maid. I started out bravely enough, came out of the locker room whistling a cheerful tune. At the door I ran into the bellboy who had given me my uniform the night before.

"Whistling to keep up your courage, kid?" he sneered.

"Could be, kid," I leaned heavily on the "kid" part.

He went on breezily, "Don't know if they told you, but you're the sixth night maid they've tried out in two weeks." He grinned, as he put his hands behind his head, "They jest don't seem to last, drop things and rattle around noisily. Big shots don't go for that. Gets them rattled. They like operators like me who are smooth and quiet. You probably won't last the night. . . ."

I guess I looked so pathetic, he decided to go easier on me. He added, almost kindly, "It ain't so bad, kid. I'm only teasing. Jest be natural and go heavy on the smilin' — don't stand cowering in the corner, like that. Be like me, talk up to the people like you knew somethin' too."

As I was riding up the freight elevator to my first floor for the evening, I thought, this must be the workers' motto at the Sea View

— talk up to them as if you knew something too. But when the elevator jerked to a stop, I couldn't think of one thing I knew to talk about, and as for being natural, I never in my life felt so wooden.

When I stepped out into the hall, the stillness unnerved me even more. When the elevator door shut behind me, it sounded like a sonic boom. I expected every door to fly open and angry faces to peer at me. I took a few faltering, stiff steps on the thick carpet, then stopped and leaned against the wall. My heart was pounding, I tried to keep telling myself — all you have to do, kid, is walk to the first door, ring the buzzer, and say pleasantly, "Night maid, may I come in?"

But I couldn't budge. I tried repeating the workers' motto, *that* I couldn't even remember. I stood as if I were a permanent wall fixture. I stared at the closed doors up and down the corridor, and at the very second when I had decided I couldn't go through with it, a door down the hall suddenly came open. Out swept an elderly couple in evening clothes. Frantically I began polishing the window of the freight elevator, and as they approached me, I leaned heavily on a smile, and at the same moment, the French routine went into action. Easily I said, "Bonsoir, madame et monsieur."

They bowed their greetings to me as they passed. I was still polishing, but less furiously. The old gentleman smiled at me and said, "You must be the new night maid."

I leaned on another smile, and as I started for their room, he slipped something in the pocket of my apron. When they disappeared around the corner, I reached in my pocket and drew out a five dollar bill. I unlocked the door to their room and entered with a swish. All was well. It wasn't only the five dollars that gave me a lift, although it surely helped. It had more to do with the smile we exchanged. With genuine satisfaction, I put their room in the best order I knew, and I left a note and a drawing on the telephone stand thanking them for their kindness.

It was the studio couches that gave me the most trouble. Happily, the lady of the room was in when I tackled the first one. She confessed that she too was not mechanically-minded. Together we figured out how the blasted thing came apart, and shared a feeling of victory when the open bed stood before us. While I made up the bed, she lined up the pillows against the wall. Then while

51

I picked up in the bathroom, she busied hereif emptying ash trays. We had the room in order in less than fifteen minutes.

Several rooms and a pocketful of bills later, I was conversing with the two ladies in room 605. We were talking about the rising cost of living. One of the ladies had just told me that the restaurant where they had had breakfast the morning before had charged them five cents extra for the second cup of coffee. I suppose you do have to economize someplace along the line when you're paying forty-five dollars a day for your room (this includes soap); well, while we were pleasantly talking, the buzzer rang, calling me to room 608.

I excused myself and ran down the hall. The door to 608 was partially open, but I knocked. A prominent movie star came and let me in. "Come in, come in," he said brightly. "Excuse me, I'm on the phone." While he ran back to the living room, he called out. "You don't have to do anything to my rooms, but I wonder if you'd be kind enough to get out some ice cubes for me?"

And so it went. I'd probably still be at the Sea View Hotel, zipping stout ladies into their formals, emptying ash trays, drawing pictures for the sad-looking guests, turning down beds and putting on the night lights, spraying the rooms so they smelled fresh and clean, and talking to the guests as if I knew something too. But with four to six hours every day at the beach, I developed an allergy to sunshine; so I had to resign. Anyway, it was about time to go home and get ready to go back to Europe.

PART TWO

Finally Switzerland

CHAPTER IX

The Beginning of a Friendship

I looked for a doorbell, but there was none. In the center of the tall, ornate door was an object which I finally decided must be the Swiss version of a doorbell. I tried pushing it. Nothing happened. Then pulling. Still no sound. At last I gave it a vigorous twist, and out came a wheezing clang.

As I stood waiting for someone to come to the door, my heart was shouting, even though I stood quietly, hardly smiling. I had waited for this moment so long, half my life; and now I was beginning my life in Switzerland, the storybook land of mountains, chalets, fern-edged trails, and Alpine horns. My family seemed far away, but actually they were not. I had left them in Sweden a few weeks ago after our trip together (they did want me to accompany them, and I had), and they would soon be sailing for the States. I thought of the good time we had shared and . . . .

Suddenly the large door swung slowly open, and a tall, thin woman in a black dress squinted at me. She spoke French. I *think* it was French, but it could have been Singhalese. The only French I was sure of was the "bonsoir, madame et monsieur" of the night maid experience the previous winter. I did not understand her, and she grasped nothing I said.

I was trying to explain that I was the "mademoiselle" who had written a few months ago reserving a room in this boarding house (pension, as they say in French). Nothing registered. I tried repeating my speech in Swedish. This was worse. Finally I reduced the whole thing to one word, "Americaine." Loudly and frequently I repeated, *"Americaine!! Americaine!!"* while pointing to myself and luggage.

A light broke.

"Ah," she said, sort of smiling.

She indicated that I was to come in. She motioned to me to sit on a wooden bench in the dark hall, and then she disappeared. As I sat in the gloomy corridor, feeling a bit homesick, I heard a few "achs" and "alors" and "ahas" coming down the hallway. Behind the tall, thin woman marched a handsome, dignified older lady leaning lightly on a cane. She looked me over rather completely, and then said, "A little English I am speaking; may I help?"

All over again I explained that I was the American who had come to live in this "pension," and so forth, and so forth. At one point she raised her cane and stopped me, "I am not with the ears hearing too well. Louder and slower, please!"

I tried again, but she still couldn't hear me, so she reached into her large, antique-brocaded bag and drew out a long, curving, silver ear trumpet. She put it to her right ear and directed me to speak into it.

For a brief moment I had a giddy feeling that *this* time I was playing a role in a musical comedy, so I sang out my part good and loud. Soon we were communicating, and communicating well, and finally I established who I was and why I was there. My new friend gave a quick command, and the maid (and a few cats which had gathered in the hallway) scampered away to get my room in order. She took me by the arm and escorted me to her room.

She was reserved with me at first, though pleasant; but when she questioned me further and learned that I had just come from Sweden on a bicycle, she threw the ear trumpet in the air, grabbed me and hugged me the way my Great-aunt Hannah used to do when she was amused.

"Bicyclette!" exclaimed Madame Dumreicher, in her deep, rich voice, "You came on a bicyclette! You Americaines, I love you. You are all quite wonderfully mad!"

"Now come," she continued, "you sit with me down and tell me all about yourself while the maid makes up your chambre."

In what seemed like a few minutes, but was actually over an hour, the maid came and timidly knocked on the door to tell Madame my room was ready. As I got up to go, Madame Dumreicher said, "I should like it very well if you will take tea with me tomorrow afternoon." She gave me a sly look; "I fix it in the room. Come around four."

As we stood by the door, she gave her cluttered, narrow, drab room a searching look. She shook her head and said, "This is a most miserable pension you have picked to live in, Mademoiselle Carlson. What is your first name? I am not liking to be formal with friends, and I am being sure we are going to be friends."

I told her my name.

She frowned, "It's not musical enough. I shall call you Bettily."

And that was the beginning of a wonderful and lasting friendship between the old German baroness and the young Americaine.

I wasn't expecting the "pension" I had picked through the mail to be first class, as I had deliberately chosen the cheapest one on the list. I had no intention of using my limited funds on room and board. I had come to Europe to see Europe.

The maid showed me to my room, and we exchanged several "alors" and "ahas" enroute down the dark stairs. My room was even smaller and more drab than Madame Dumreicher's, and it had bars on the window. It was below the street level with the sidewalk right alongside the window. I couldn't have cared less. I was thrilled to be in Switzerland, and would cheerfully have accepted accommodations in the city jail. But there was no law saying I had to remain in my room all the time; so I left the heap of luggage in the center of the room, and walked on the Avenue de la Rumine until I came to a small park.

Lausanne is built on seven levels. Our "pension" was on about the third or fourth terrace, so the view from the park was splendid. My eyes swept across Lake Geneva to the Savoy Alps and on around to the vineyards. I looked at the flowers all around me, the weeping willows, the neat holly hedge. I sat and enjoyed it for nearly an hour. Then I returned to my barred cell and unpacked.

CHAPTER X

Two for Tea and
Some Cats

Madame Dumreicher was right. I had picked a miserable "pension." It was mostly an old folks' home and a refuge for cats. I got along fine with the old folks, that is, *most* of them, but the cats! Cats are like harpsichord music or tomato juice for breakfast they make me uneasy and squeamish.

The first dinner in the "pension" is worth mentioning. Actually, it was supper, because in Switzerland they have dinner at noon. Distinctly I recall it was night. The supper hour was late, about 7:30, and the lights were on in the dining room. It was the dimness that was intriguing. Five-watt bulbs, hidden under enormous, floppy lamp shades that looked like giant mushrooms or hats in the Gay Nineties, issued forth a mere suggestion of light. It was not only the Mademoiselle who ran our "pension" who liked soft lighting, but all Swiss. I do not believe the average Swiss can tolerate anything stronger than twenty-five watts, and this is true all over Europe.

Most Europeans would be blinded if they walked unwarned into the typical American home. As I groped my way into the dining room, I was hoping I would see Madame Dumreicher. Finally, I made out her imposing figure across the room. An elderly man was shouting something into her ear trumpet in a language I had never heard. Madame Dumreicher reached out her hand to me as I stumbled towards her.

"Ach, it is so dark in here, I am not recognizing you," she said.
She introduced me to several people standing in the shadow be-

hind us. She also explained that the man to whom she was speaking was from Cairo. "As I started to tell you this afternoon," she said, "many years of my life were spent in Egypt."

The language they were speaking was Arabic. As others gathered, the noise increased. Madame Dumreicher indicated that she was putting away her ear trumpet. "We can talk afterwards," she shouted. "I am not liking all the confusion."

The maid came and showed me my place at the large center table. Once we were seated, I was on my own. Madame Dumreicher was at the far end of the table, and with her deafness and the darkness, I couldn't possibly communicate with her.

Gradually my eyes became accustomed to the *soft* lighting, and so I looked around. There were ten or twelve of us at the main table. In one corner of the room, partially hidden behind a large potted plant, sat a woman in a fluttery chiffon dress. Never did I learn why she sat at this private table. As one of my friends would say, "She's the exclusive type." Perhaps. Her hair was marcelled in tight, perfect waves, and around her neck was a long chain of black beads which occasionally she tossed back dramatically. I had a fine opportunity to study her, because frequently she would peek around the potted plant, hold up her lorgnette and examine in detail each one of us at the center table; and particularly me, as I was the newest specimen.

The two little, very old ladies who sat directly across from me had shuffled into the room and gone immediately to their places and sat down. I do not think they had the strength to stand. Next to them sat a talkative, elderly man with a beard. He was forever asking me questions, in French, of course. All I could do was smile and nod my head.

Had I known then it was going to take me six months to pass beyond the grinning and head-shaking stage, I do not believe I would have had the fortitude to stick it out. Not knowing what people are saying to you is worse than frustrating. When an entire group bursts into laughter after you've tried to say something, you naturally suspect they are laughing at you. It took all the courage I had to smile along with others. The muscles around my mouth ached those first few months in Switzerland from forcing myself to smile through conversations in which I had not the slightest idea what was being said.

At the head of our table sat the owner of the "pension," a strange, in-another-world person; I'll call her Mademoiselle Gaunt. She adored cats, far more than her boarders. The favorite cat sat in her lap throughout the supper, and she kept feeding several others which bounded in and out of the door leading to the terrace.

Twice a cat inadvertently jumped upon the table. The second time, regrettably for the cat, it landed in the vicinity of Madame Dumreicher. She took a wide swing at the animal with her cane, missed, but sent a bottle of red wine flying to the floor with a crash that caused the potted plant lady to go into a spasm of hysterical coughing. She had just taken a sip of the spicy soup, which in itself was getting a snuffle out of the best of us; and when Madame Dumreicher went into action it caught her in the midst of swallowing. The cat leaped from the table and out the door, and I don't recall that I ever again saw *that* cat, certainly not on the table. When we all passed the startled stage, a roar of laughter went up. There were two, however, who did not even smile politely, Mlle Gaunt and the Mlle of the Potted Plant.

I looked down the table at my new friend with increased interest. She did not have to say she was an aristocrat. You knew it. Normally, she was dignified and refined, a real lady; but she had a streak of imp in her that, in the years I knew her, was forever throwing people into an uproar. No, I'm not so sure it was imp. It was more a doing of the spontaneous, right thing. The cat had no business on the table. She saw it, disliked what she saw, and with her cane handy, she did what she could.

For a lady who had lived a complex and tragic life, I marveled at her simplicity and directness. She was always herself, never out of character, and the same with everybody. I imagine had this situation come up in the days when she was dining in banquet rooms, she would have acted the same. She would have swished the intruder off the table, missing it, of course, and sending a shower of crystal goblets and gold decanters into the lap of a duchess. She would have accomplished her purpose. The cat would never jump on a table again, and the duchess would have forgiven her. There is joy in forgiving people who err as splendidly as Madame Dumreicher.

There was only one other young person at the table besides myself, and that was a handsome Greek who sat next to me. He enjoyed teasing. It is painful enough to be kidded in your own language, but this was torture. The set smile got stiffer and stiffer. If there was a lull in the conversation, Monsieur the Greek would turn to me and say,

"Parlez, Mademoiselle, parlez, parlez!" (Speak, speak).

Happily, there were not many lulls. These people adored talking, and several languages were being spoken at once. It got noisier and noisier. I was wishing I had an ear trumpet to put away. Most of the old folks were hard of hearing, so there was much repeating and shouting. At the height of the shrill talk, the lady behind the potted plant stepped from behind her plant, and with a magnificent gesture, screeched above the roar,

"Silence! Attention, attention, tout le monde!"

To my astonishment, "tout le monde" became quiet. I mean, everybody. In the silence, she walked to the radio by her table, turned the dial, and as we all sat holding our breath, she listened to the news.

When I went to have tea with Madame Dumreicher on the following afternoon, she greeted me with her twinkling eyes and stern face, "Well, what are you thinking? Have you ever been in a situation like this?"

I had to admit it was different.

She escorted me into her narrow, crowded room and saw that I was comfortable with several pillows behind me on her couch. She sat in the old leather rocking chair by the tea table. Even though we drank our tea from chipped cups, and the paper on the wall I was facing was stained and peeling, Madame Dumreicher created her own atmosphere. Taking tea with my grand old German friend was the one thing I looked forward to more than anything else during my first year in Switzerland.

We often sat for hours talking, sharing our lives. She learned to love my family in a genuine way. She was always interested in the latest news. Part of it was the fact that she believed largely in love and loyalty. Many times she said, "Family and friends should stand together, no matter what." The two world wars had plowed through her life and scarred or destroyed every sacred relationship she had known. "Forty years I am on top," she said once, "and forty years I am coming down.

"The first time I am coming to Lausanne from Egypt, I am com-

61

ing with my good and gentle husband. We were arriving only for a little holiday with twenty large trunks, our servants . . . ." She looked around the dingy room. "Ach, now be looking, all that is left is boxes, these funny little boxes."

She always referred to the cheap suitcases lined against the wall as boxes. It wasn't only that Madame Maria von Dumreicher had gone from large trunks to little boxes — that is an old, tired story in Europe. What was amazing about her, in spite of all the crushing tragedy, was that she had never completely lost her love for living, a sparkle which few people have even in the best of circumstances. What drew me to the old baroness was her spirit and that delightful childlike heart of hers which made all those who knew her, love and respect her.

CHAPTER XI

Go Straight Ahead!

Madame Dumreicher told me it was not difficult to find the Lausanne Music Conservatory. "Look for the Black Cat Restaurant, 'Le Chat Noir,' then, Allez tout droit, tout droit, tout droit!"

This is a common French expression. You might as well learn it now. Sooner or later you will come across it if you venture into a French-speaking nation or book. It means simply, "Go straight ahead," but the part that is baffling for those of us new at the game, the French have a maddening way of repeating words and phrases. It is never simply, "Allez tout droit," but a spasm of "tout droit's," and when you are first learning the language and hanging on to every syllable, you end up thinking the Music Conservatory is north of Paris. But finally I located it, after going "tout droit" down the wrong street, a grave mistake in Lausanne. At the bottom of the steep hill, I found a gendarme who spoke better English than I do, and he sent me back up the same hill.

There were several other Americans enrolled at the Conservatory, many British students, and practically all the faculty knew English, a deplorable situation as far as learning French is concerned. But it made it easy to get enrolled and started.

As I began filling out forms, the registrar looked over my record. "I see you've played the oboe for many years," she commented. "We have another American here, studying the oboe."

I cleared my throat, "I realize it sounds odd, but I'm not going on with the oboe."

By this time I knew myself well enough to realize I would always be traveling, and the oboe does not endear itself to people when practiced in hotel rooms or "pensions"; and as there is no other way to play an oboe well except to blow into it every day, I knew I had come to the end of something else dear in my life. To be sure I wouldn't weaken and be talked into "keeping it up," I gave away my oboe in Norway.

It was at the Music Conservatory that Bernie and Charlie came into my life. Bernie, the oboist, was from Colorado, and Charlie, who played both the flute and viola, was from North Carolina. We did not have much to do the first few days of registration, and so we got acquainted with the tea rooms of Lausanne and one another.

European tea rooms are something the U.S.A. could use more of. They are as tastefully furnished as many hotel bars, only they do not have the dark atmosphere. The lighting is soft (typical Swiss lighting), but sufficiently bright so you can see the oil paintings on the walls and recognize your friends when they enter. The tea rooms have the intimacy and charm of the former drugstore, only they are more comfortable.

Mutreux's was "tout droit" from the Conservatory if you were heading downtown, and we always seemed to be heading that way, at least those first few days. One morning over our expresso Bernie, Charlie and I were telling about where we were living in Lausanne. They were laughing about my "pension" of cats and old people. I had reached the stage where I wasn't laughing; stepping on cats' tails in dark corridors no longer amused me.

"We've got the best setup," Bernie said, "real home living and no cats!"

"Right off our room there's a balcony with the lake, the Savoy Alps, everything gorgeous to feast your eyes on," Charlie added, rolling his eyes at the "coupe de fraise," the waitress just brought him, a beautifully decorated strawberry sundae with a wafer balanced on top of the whipped cream.

The only view from my window with the bars was the lower part of peoples' legs as they walked by and a few dogs and cats which peered in.

"There's only one thing wrong at our place," Charlie said, "Fred!"

Bernie clapped his hand on his head, "He's a character, a real gone guy. The other night he started practicing about two — two in the morning!"

Charlie explained, "Madame Robert as politely as she knew told the nut to shut up, but he didn't get it why he shouldn't play when he was *moved* to play." Charlie looked thoughtful, "Bernie, Fred has to go. That's all there's to it. He's gotta go. Now, with the right motivation, we ought to be able to convince him that *Paris* is the place for an artist of his sensitivity."

I did not know Charlie very well then, but soon I came to know with the others that when Charlie set his mind to something, heaven help the one he had decided to "motivate."

A few weeks after our talk about Fred at Mutreux's, someone knocked on my practice room door at the Conservatory. My progress with the piano was nearly as poor as with French. I had played a solo instrument too long and could think only one note at a time, so when Bernie suggested a coffee break, I was ready to leave.

"I've got good news," Bernie said grinning. "Fred's going to Paris!" He looked at his watch. "In fact, he's gone. Charlie was seeing him off on the five o'clock express for Paris."

While we were waiting for our coffee, Bernie continued, "Here's the deal. We've been telling Madame Robert about you, leading up to it, sort of, you know, bringing in the sordid details of the dump you live in, the cats, the stuff they serve for soup, and mentioning what a refined, quiet person you are. . . ."

"Great scott, you didn't have to go *that* far!"

"You'll get on fine with Madame Robert," he said, ignoring me. "She is kind and nice, even though quite Swiss, and I've seen her laugh at Charlie until the tears ran down her cheeks." He warned me, "She'll be reserved at first, but I think when she gets to know you, she'll change her mind."

"What do you mean, change her mind?"

"Well, she prefers fellows," Bernie hastened to add. "Nothing personal, but she said that women are more of a problem in a house than men. They take so much time in the bathroom putting up their hair, and . . . . Well, anyway, Charlie assured her that you would be no more trouble than we are; of course, that's not saying much, but what I'm getting at, Madame Robert has consented to, at least, meet you. I told her we'd bring you around tonight right after supper, OK?"

"Yik!" I said, not feeling "refined and quiet," and wondering if I'd pass the test. I was moved by the thoughtfulness of these fellows. It's difficult to find a decent place in Lausanne, because of the many students who live in "pensions." I had gone as far as I could with the cats and barred room, no heat and little light. Nothing was holding me there. Only the week before, we had found a large, sunny room in another "pension" for Madame Dumreicher; and the only pet in the large, three-story house was one small canary. "Birds I am liking," she said, "but cats — ach! I move with no regrets; you too must leave this unbearable place, Schatzi."

And so two weeks after the Baroness moved with "no regrets," I gleefully said farewell to the cats, Mlle Gaunt and the dark, dreary boarding house.

CHAPTER XII

One Happy, Noisy Family

M adame Robert and I liked each other from the beginning. So
the following week the boys helped me pick up my few belongings, and I moved in with the Robert family. That was the start-
ing point of a merry, wild, hilarious, joyful, sad, very sad, unforgettable two years. It is odd about some people: even though they
travel thousands of miles from home, they still want to be at home.
Bernie, Charlie and I shared this oddness, plus our love for music,
hot dogs, Switzerland, good times, coffee, talking, and friendly people. We found a little bit of all at Madame Robert's.

Without the benefit of color and sound, it's difficult to give a
true picture of what it was like living in that apartment on one of
the high terraces in Lausanne, overlooking Lake Geneva, the French
Alps, the vineyards and the Port of Pully. How Madame Robert
stood it (the noise, particularly), I'll never know. Yes, I do know
today, but I didn't then. She was and is a woman of strong, quiet
faith. When her missionary husband was killed accidentally in
Madagascar early in their marriage, she determined, with the help
of God, to raise her three children as he would have wanted them
to grow up. It takes money to feed, clothe, and educate the young,
so she did what she could by giving piano lessons and renting out
rooms to music students.

The music alone in the three-bedroom apartment, to quote
twelve-year-old Daniel, was "formidable." As I have told you, Bernie played the oboe, Charlie, the flute and viola, Jacqueline, Madame Robert's daughter, was studying the piano. Then there was
five-year-old Nicolette, from London, who, along with me, was
learning the fundamentals of the piano, plus Madame Robert's practicing and a steady stream of pupils; and, when Daniel could be

forced to stand still for a half hour, he played the violin. It was a wild and wonderful place to live, and not one cat.

One day, as I walked up the two flights of stairs to the apartment, immediately I sensed that something "extraordinaire" was going on. There was no noise. I unlocked the door with apprehension. As I was carrying a pile of books and music, I had to kick shut the heavy Swiss door with my foot. Normally the slamming of a door in this noise-drenched musician's haven was like dropping a hand wrench in a riveting section of the Navy Yard, but on this day the bang echoed throughout the solid, old building.

Jacqueline rushed into the hall, and whispered,

"Silence, silence. We must be quiet. Mother's had a letter that there's too much noise here." She, of course, spoke French, but such words as "silence" and "lettre" do not need interpretation; but to get the details, I knocked on Bernie and Charlie's door and asked in a normal voice, "What's going on?"

You would have thought that I had screamed the question. They made wild motions for me to come in, while Charlie eased shut the door behind me. Bernie shoved on the floor a stack of Winston Salem newspapers, so I could sit down while they told me what had happened.

I better explain that besides the three of us *and* Madame Robert *and* her three children *and* Nicolette, there were always extra boarders for dinner and supper, plus a cook *and* a series of maids. We wore out maids faster than oboe reeds. Madame Robert always warned the girls that there was some practicing going on, and they would reply cheerfully that they liked music; but within a month, a week, once even a day, however, it would develop that they had a sick relative who needed immediate attention, or they were making an unexpected trip to Outer Mongolia. The practicing would continue, maid or no maid, regular meals or irregular. Nothing daunted us until the letter came.

Bernie, Charlie, and I had mentioned our admiration for the Swiss and their ability to take it. Being Americans, we were familiar with apartment regulations: "No dogs, no children, no cats, positively no musical instruments." Our jolly combination would have lasted in an American apartment only long enough to get the riot squad there.

The letter upset Madame Robert. Apartments were difficult to find in post-war Europe. The boys said that she was now in the studio-living room working out a schedule for us, and that she wanted absolute silence the rest of the day. The apartment manager had written that the man who lived below us had complained of hearing (at one time) two pianos, one violin, one flute, one oboe, one trombone, and a chorus of children screaming. Charlie was quick to point out that there was little truth in the matter, as not one of us played a trombone. As if seeing a light, he added, "I must be getting a deep, rich sound out of my viola."

Soberly we discussed the subject, and then drifted into swapping stories. At first we were careful to control noise, but after a spell of laughing into pillows, Charlie let loose. He calmed down only after someone opened the door and a hand waved the letter at us.

Later as I walked down the hall to my room, I continued thinking about our life with the Robert family, the feeling of oneness we already shared. This was no ordinary Swiss "pension," this was home to us.

Bernie arrived in Lausanne first. He had been stationed in the Army in Germany at the close of the war, and had spent a furlough in Switzerland. That was all he needed to be convinced he would return some day. After his discharge, he went back to the University of Colorado to finish his degree. By the spring of 1948 he was on the way back to Europe with a few coins jingling in his pocket. These he had earned waiting on tables in a fraternity house.

When he registered at the Music Conservatory, the secretary gave him a list of approved "pensions." He walked along the Avenue de la Rumine until he came to a small, terraced park, the same one I had discovered. It was a cold, windy day. It was a "bise" day. This is a particularly penetrating wind that blows off the high mountains now and then.

As Bernie walked down the steps into the park, he noticed how much warmer it was. The garden section where there were benches was set back into the hill, sheltered from the "bise." Bernie sat down and let the sun warm his long, lean frame while he enjoyed the view. After a while he pulled out the list of addresses he had in his pocket. The closest one to the park was Madame Robert. He smiled, "That's for me." When he was shown a room facing the same view, he needed little convincing. That afternoon he moved in.

Charlie was a friend of Bernie's at the University of Colorado, and so when Bernie began writing enthusiastic letters about Switzerland, Charlie started packing his bag. He delighted in explaining to all of us why he came to Lausanne: "I came to keep an eye on Bernie. You got to watch out for oboe players." So that is how the Robert family got Charlie, and when you have Charlie, as Madame Robert said, you have something!

Jacqueline, when she learned that an American was going to live with them, went and hid. Her idea of Americans, based on two films and what her brother Daniel had told her, was something to run from. The supper bell brought her out of hiding, however, and she was forced to meet the "horrid" American. And there stood nice, kind Bernie, six feet four and very thin. She expected him to be fat, loud and smoking a long, black cigar.

During the first few days, Bernie was painfully shy. He had studied French, but at the beginning he was speechless. He did answer one direct question Daniel put to him, "How old are you?"

Bernie answered, "Quatre-vingts ans." He reversed the "quatre" and "vingt," and instead of saying "twenty-four," he said "eighty." He continued to have stormy sessions with the language those first few months, but after a while, he worked out a routine that did wonders for his speech. It was a fifteen-minute walk from the Conservatory to the apartment; and so, every day while he was walking home for dinner, he would prepare in his mind three things that he was going to say at the table. He'd walk along muttering his three French sentences over and over. As soon as the table grace was spoken, and before anyone else had a chance to open his mouth, Bernie would break forth with his three prepared sentences. By the time Charlie moved in, Bernie was conversing pleasantly with the family and other boarders and could join in on all the laughs over Charlie's first wild attempts at speaking French.

The French Charlie spoke was something which when you have once heard it, you will never forget. It was spoken with a Southern accent and was an untamed mixture of mispronounced English words, a smattering of French verbs and nouns, and a broad range of colorful adjectives and expletives which he had picked up from

70

Daniel. But Charlie was a gifted story teller, and he never let a small thing like a language barrier stand in his way.

The competition was fierce between Charlie and Daniel to control the conversation at meals, and what with Bernie and his prepared remarks (he was up to ten sentences a meal by the time I moved in), and with all the others around the table and their fluency in French, I never did learn to speak French well. I consoled myself with the knowledge that every group needs a good listener, and I learned to listen well in French.

Charlie was a paradox: a clown at heart but also a serious and dedicated musician. His knowledge of music was remarkable; and he was also an excellent performer. Then he enjoyed composing. We had an agreement that whenever I was not in my room, he could use my piano. Several afternoons when I would come back from classes, I'd find Charlie in his faded blue dungarees, a blue and white striped robe, a towel wrapped around his neck, and barefooted, huddled over the piano working on harmony.

It didn't surprise me when I was listening to my car radio while driving across Wisconsin several years later to hear Charlie playing in a woodwind quintet.

The bathing situation at Madame Robert's did present some problems. There was one bathroom, about the size of an ordinary closet, for the nine or ten of us living there, and we had hot water once a week. Having hot water only on Saturdays helped ease the weekly traffic.

One Saturday Charlie missed his hot water bath. It was the main topic of conversation at Sunday dinner. He seemed indifferent, but finally we worked it out of him how he could afford to miss his bath of the week. "Alors," he said, "J'ai baigné aujourd'hui à la guerre." A typical Charlie sentence. He meant to say that he had bathed at the railroad station, but what he said was, "I bathed today in the war." However he said it, he had made a wonderful discovery. It changed our lives. He explained to us, "I bet you didn't know they have showers at the station, with an unlimited supply of hot water. One franc with soap and towel, but if you bring your own, it's only fifty centimes." He added, "It's real clean, and there is the nicest lady who takes your money." He turned to Madame Robert and me, "And you'd like it too."

Bernie frowned at him. Charlie glared back.

71

"You imbécile," he said to Bernie, "There's a special place for les dames!" At the same time, he smiled happily at Daniel ("imbécile was one of his favorites), our young language professor, who was helping us increase our vocabulary.

After Charlie's great discovery, it was not a rare sight, during the middle of the week or the night, to see Charlie, Bernie, and myself off for "la gare" with towels around our necks and soap in our pockets. It was nice to have unlimited hot water again, but regrettably, it took the zest out of hot water Saturdays. During the height of the winter, about the only exercise we got was the brisk walk between the apartment and the Conservatory and the apartment and the railroad station.

CHAPTER XIII

My Friend, Jean Paul

O n one of my first days at Madame Robert's, I was called to the front door. A businesslike woman spoke French to me for several minutes before I could interrupt and tell her I didn't understand a word she said. When I heard the giggles coming from Jacqueline's room, I caught on. She and a friend had told the saleslady that I was the lady of the house and very much interested in buying a vacuum cleaner.

As you do not need much language to bawl out children, I pretended to be angry about the trick they had played on me. Our friendship blossomed quickly when they learned I was good material for tricking.

Jacqueline was about ten when I moved in, and she was the only person anywhere, any time, with whom I conversed easily in French. She spoke in a flowing way, and if I indicated that I wasn't following her, she would illustrate or act out what she was saying. Then too she would supply me with the words I was groping for, so our conversations moved right along.

She had already lived a couple of lives, even though she was still a child. In the previous ten years the Robert family had lived on two continents, been through a revolution, suffered much loss, and lived in a chalet in the Alps, before moving to Lausanne. She had one unfulfilled ambition. Jacqueline had always wanted a sister, and even though I was considerably older than what she had wanted, she adopted me. Besides, it fortified her to have another woman in the house. She was at the age when brothers are hard to take; with Bernie, Charlie, and the boarders too, she lived a tormented life.

The chief torturer was Daniel. Often when Jacqueline and I

were talking, he'd be lurking about, pretending he wasn't the least interested in us. One day he could not hold silence,

"Jacqueline, c'est formidable!" (Everything was formidable to him.) "How do you expect your pupil to learn French," he shouted, "if you do not correct her? Imbécile, idiote, stupide . . . !"

He had heard me say, "Adieu," to a friend when I was seeing her out the door. "You must never say 'adieu' to a person you are going to meet again," he said, his small, dynamic body all animation and gestures. " 'Adieu' means, well . . ." he shrugged his shoulders, waved his hands, "to be exact" (and Daniel loved to be *exact*) " 'adieu' means 'until we meet with God.' "

The lesson continued, while Jacqueline amused herself by imitating her brother behind his back. " 'Au revoir' is what we French say," he said with authority. "It means, 'Until we meet again.' "

It was rarely dull at the Robert's, but lest I mislead you, we, too, had moments of quiet dignity. It was during one of the coffee hours that Madame Robert told us Jean Paul was coming home for Christmas. We three Americans thoroughly enjoyed the coffee hour. In Switzerland they allow two hours at noon for dinner; the banks, post offices, and stores close; we found it a fine and noble custom.

After dinner with fruit for dessert, we would always go into the living room and have coffee. Often we would listen to music; sometimes, just talk. On occasion we would have after-dinner music with the talent we had in the room. On days after you'd been up late at night, it was quite proper to take a nap.

As I said before, it was at one of the coffee hours that Madame Robert told me about Jean Paul. She had mentioned to all of us that he was coming home for Christmas. Then when Bernie went off to take a nap, Charlie to do some silent practicing, and the children went out to play, she told me more about her seventeen-year-old son.

"He is not well," she said quietly, "not at all well, and it will be tense while he is home. Jacqueline and Daniel are too young to understand. They think I favor him and they get upset. He is frail and does require attention, but because he is so brave and cheerful, they don't understand how ill he is."

Gently she added, "I believe you and Jean Paul will understand one another. Because of all my pupils, I do not have time to talk

74

with him as I ought, and he desperately needs someone to visit with him, to listen to him, and try to understand his struggle."

From the beginning, Jean Paul and I did enjoy talking. He was studying English in Geneva and was delighted to practice. I was delighted to speak English. It was like embracing an old, reliable friend. There was an unwritten law in the apartment that French was always to be spoken, but on the afternoons when Jean Paul and I sat on the balcony and the others had scattered, we had some unforgettable long talks. In English.

On one occasion, Jean Paul turned directly to me and said calmly, "Maman told you that I have cancer, didn't she?"

He said it in a quiet, matter-of-fact way, the way you might tell a friend, my mother told you, didn't she, that I plan to take a trip to Japan next summer. No, his mother had not told me. We had never discussed the nature of his illness. She had merely implied that it was serious. We sat silently for a moment looking at the view. We both loved sunshine, the mountains, and the blue lake. We were bundled up well in coats, scarves, and blankets. Charlie had put up a crude but effective shelter on the balcony, to keep off the December wind, so when the sun reached us, it was a grand place to be.

We had discussed many things in the few days we had known each other: favorite books and music, different countries we had visited, Charlie, Bernie, my family in America, his father who had been killed, how much we loved mountains, the French comedian Fernandel, and radishes sliced on fresh bread and butter. We had talked about many things, but never his illness.

I had come to love the gentle, wise lad, even in this short time. Jean Paul did not have the robustness of his brother or sister; nevertheless, he was intensely alive, quick to catch things, and deep spiritually, in a light, detached way, as if he had insight that some one was in control, not only of his life, but the whole world.

Guardedly I explained that his mother had not told me the nature of his illness. With scarcely a pause, he asked in the same quiet, calm voice, "Betty, do you ever think about death?"

The question pierced me at my most vulnerable point. I never thought about death. I never let it enter my thinking. I had no answers, and so I dealt with the great, dark, real shadow in a "splendidly" neurotic way. I simply did not think about it. It is not easy,

75

but possible for awhile, particularly if death does not get too personal. Also it helps if you keep very, very busy and allow little time for the questions without answers; and, eventually, what you do not think about does not disturb you, that is, on the surface. It only eats at you from underneath, and tears you apart when confronting you directly in a situation like this. All I could do was shake my head and look away from the earnest, young face and murmur that I'd think about it at some later date.

One of the many things that had attracted me to Jean Paul was his quiet strength. I couldn't put my finger on it, but there was something unusual about him. I sensed he knew something I did not know. What he said next was totally incomprehensible to me at the time. With dignity and kindness he said, "You need not fear to think of death. It can be almost a friend."

Suddenly Daniel banged open the door to the balcony to tell us in an excited voice that his mother was beginning the Christmas preparations, and we were all forbidden to go into the dining or living room. That was the end of our serious conversation; but once Jean Paul had planted the question in my mind and his unusual observations about death, nothing could shut off my thinking about it. Since my days in Europe had begun, I had gone along quite well without letting the questions about God, life, war, purpose, suffering, hunger, and death overwhelm me. But the one question, "Do you ever think about death?" made me more restless than ever.

CHAPTER XIV

Adieu

I entered the Christmas holidays with more determination than ever to be happy and forget the gnawing ache inside. They were special days. Madame Robert went all out to make this a memorable occasion for her three children and the Americans sharing her home.

There was mystery and suspense in the apartment, and when the doors were finally opened to the festive rooms Madame Robert had spent hours decorating, we were all in high spirits. After we had enjoyed a delicious Christmas supper, complete with the Swiss Yule log as centerpiece, which turned out to be tasty mocha chocolate cake, we went into the colorful, cheerful living room. Before Daniel was given permission to light the candles on the small, lovely tree, we gathered near the piano and sang Christmas hymns.

Singing is like praying. When you do it, you do it in the language you love best, the one you learned as a child. Suddenly I realized that we were singing in different tongues. Madame Robert in German, the children in French, and I don't have to tell you what the three Americans were singing. When we came to "Adeste Fideles," Charlie, who directed the choir at the Scottish Church, added Latin to our ensemble. It was a hushed and beautiful moment, one of those rare times you wish you could hold on to forever; and, years later, you realize that you have. I saw Madame Robert steal a glance at Jean Paul. His radiant, flushed face returned a wonderful smile.

After the exchanging of gifts and a Christmas program with each of us participating, we all went to church together. Charlie, who was rarely subtle, kept shaking his head during the entire brisk walk to Place St. François, muttering. "Never thought I'd see you two birds in church!"

He was paying homage to Bernie and me. We believed somewhat the same, that all religions are good, and the man of culture and education embraces all of them. We went to church occasionally, Bernie and I, because we loved beautiful music, and you sometimes hear it in church; but we never wished to be so provincial as to go to the same church Sunday after Sunday.

We had some of our best talks on Sunday mornings when all the others had gone to church. Recently I had become interested in the Moral Rearmament Movement, and had spent a few weekends at their Swiss headquarters at Caux, up above Montreux. Even Madame Robert got into some of those discussions, as we were still going strong through the Sunday dinner. As I try to retrace in my mind the conversation now, one sentence stands out. "They are missing one thing," she said, "the authentic Christ."

We discussed it at length. "So what if Christ is left out?" I said. "What has he to do with the matter anyway?"

Then Bernie and I enjoyed discussing philosophy. Emerson was a favorite of Bernie, and Thoreau was the one who got to me the most. He never accepted truth second hand. Once he said, "Heaven is under our feet as well as over our head," and he learned it by experiencing it when he lived unencumbered in the New England woods. Bernie and I wrestled hard with the thinking of many of these men, and we nearly convinced ourselves we were growing in wisdom and stature; but ironically, God, peace, and a quiet mind seemed always to be beyond. It was as if our "wisdom" was only the mountains we saw directly before us from the balcony.

After the holidays, Jean Paul went back to school in Geneva. He was physically unable to carry a full load, but he accomplished what he could, and this seemed to mean much to him. Life went on somewhat the same in the apartment. The noisy, enthusiastic practicing was resumed. Happily, the gardener beneath us had found a quiet apartment in another neighborhood, and the family that moved in had several children and a barking dog. The pleasant coffee hours, discussions, and musicals went on, and we all kept busy with classes to attend, French verbs to conjugate, and hot showers to take at the railroad station. Jacqueline continued to teach me French, and Daniel continued to correct both of us.

It was in the spring that Daniel and I broke through to solid friendship. He didn't warm up to foreigners quickly, and to add to the disadvantages, I was "une dame." Daniel's great passion was to own a racing bicycle, and being a bike lover myself, I helped him convince his skeptical mother that a deluxe racing bicycle was just what he needed. He would study harder, behave better, and practice longer, if he could fulfill his heart's desire. He got the bike.

To show his undying gratitude, he let me accompany him on one or two Saturday trips. I came back a physical wreck, but warmed inside in a special way. Daniel was fighting battles those days too. He was trying to be the man of the house, a big order for a boy, and so much of the noise that came out of him was his way of showing authority. A sort of crazy, wonderful, mutual admiration society sprang up between us. I started taking his part when everybody descended upon him, and he defended me if anybody dared to laugh at my French.

There came a day late in the spring when it was time for me to return to the United States. Jean Paul had an operation in April, and a few weeks later he came to the apartment to convalesce. He rallied very well after the surgery, and so when I left to go home, I went off with a light heart. Jean Paul was better, I was planning to come back in the fall, and we'd all pick up and go on from where we had left off.

Madame Dumreicher had provided for my flight a basketful of Swiss cheeses and sausages, biscuits, chocolate, fruit, and I can't remember what else. She had no confidence that I'd be fed between Lausanne, Switzerland, and Rockford, Illinois, and far be it from me to spoil her fun by telling her that Swiss Air is noted for its seven-course dinners.

There was a pleasant buzz of commotion in the railroad station. The Robert children came to see me off. Jacqueline called out several times, "Au revoir," and in English, "Come queeckly back."

"Au revoir" was ringing up and down the platform as people hung out of the train windows to get a last glimpse of their friends. I looked at Jean Paul with his thin, white face smiling above his thick, turtleneck sweater. We were all enjoying the foolish antics of Daniel who was pretending to shed tears into a bottle. In the midst of the fun, the train started to glide out of the station. Jean Paul made a quick reach for my hand. Our eyes met for a second as his hand was jerked out of mine when the train surged forward. The last words were his, "Adieu, chère Betty, adieu."

Within three hours my plane took off from Geneva, right when the ticket said it would. The Swiss take pride in punctuality. We circled the blue-green lake, and suddenly, there in front of us, in all majesty and splendor, stood the whole range of snow-capped Alps with pinnacles reaching into heaven in an attitude of praise. As I stared in wonder and awe, I kept hearing in my heart Jean Paul's poignant farewell. After we passed an unbelievably beautiful orchid and gold cloud castle and finally rose above the mountains, above the clouds, I closed my eyes. But the boyish, gentle face could not be erased. I prayed silently and in agony the first honest prayer I had uttered since a child. "Why, God, why are you taking his life and leaving behind some one like me?" I pressed my forehead hard against the icy window and sobbed noiselessly.

The black-edged envelope announcing the death of Jean Paul Robert came the last part of the summer. A few days later, my faithful friend, Madame Dumreicher penned these words:

"Truly, it was extraordinaire. You are knowing, Schatzi, the nurse who is coming twice the week to me to give shots for the blood pressure that shoots up, Sister Didie? Well, she is spending the last days with Jean Paul. She is saying to me, he was magnifique. All the time, the last days, he is sitting in the large, comfortable 'fauteuil,' how you saying in English, chair with arms? He is sitting in your room looking out to the mountains. In his lap he is holding his Bible, and in his heart, strong faith.

"He did suffer, oh, yes, in bad pain, Soeur Didie is saying, but his courage is not failing. To his mother he nods all is well. Soeur Didie is telling me that she is never seeing so stalwart a Christian in such a young man."

To believe in God, or more precisely, to believe God, is harder, much harder, for some than others. I shall always have special kinship with doubters, because I was one so long. Almost two years after the death of Jean Paul, I met another family in Switzerland, an American family who lived in a chalet in the Alps. Some people are better able to put things into words than others, and this is the great treasure this family has. They helped me to understand that a faith like Jean Paul's is not an exclusive possession; even I could experience his quiet trust, his quiet mind, if . . . but I am going ahead of the story.

Nineteen forty-nine and 1950 were years of surface contentment. Through Madame Dumreicher I met Carol, a brilliant student from New York City, who helped interest me in psychoanalysis. "How do you expect to write?" she said one night when we were at the Black Cat cafe enjoying thin-sliced salami sandwiches with the hottest pickles I've ever tasted, "if you don't know yourself?"

She went on to explain that all her writer friends in Greenwich Village had been psychoanalyzed. I argued a little, pondered some, and decided maybe Carol had something. A small amount of progress had been made in my life. Finally, I had decided what I wanted to be: a writer. But the more I thought about who I am, and what I have to say, I thought, yes, who am I and what do I have to say?

Before we went to Paris for a few days, Carol wrote to a friend in New York to suggest the name of a qualified analyst in Lausanne, preferably not the most expensive. When we returned from our holiday, the answer had arrived. Off I went to get acquainted with myself.

The analyst and I did not make any startling discoveries about me, but the time was not wasted. The doctor was a lovely, refined woman who had studied art in Paris in her younger days. I thoroughly enjoyed talking to her a couple of times every week. She did get out of me the fact that there was an emptiness at the core of my being, but she had nothing to fill in, other than to say it was there. And so another year went by, and back to Switzerland I went in the autumn of 1950 after a stimulating summer as a counselor at a camp on the edge of Lake Geneva, Wisconsin.

PART THREE

Found in Switzerland

Introduction to Part III

When I first sent "The Unhurried Chase" to a publisher years ago, it was mailed back to me directly with a letter explaining, "We are a *religious* publishing house."

I knew they were a *religious* publishing house. It was exactly why I had sent my story to them about two fun-loving, somewhat artistic, and occasionally ridiculous creatures who had been stuck in a Swiss chalet for a couple of weeks with a pack of missionaries. Something was bound to happen, and it did. So I wrote about what happened, being one of the two creatures, and sent the story to the publisher, being under the impression that religion had something to do with God and people getting together, regardless how ridiculous the people.

When the manuscript was shot back to me, I left it in a box in the basement to gather moss and lichen while I grew older and more experienced with publishers. I was also going to add, "and wiser," but that is carrying it too far.

In the following years, to keep my life as uncomplicated as possible, I decided to follow one teacher. Having had so many, so long, and ending up so muddled, it was refreshing to listen to one clear voice. As it turned out, it proved to be a wise choice. But I have to admit, wisdom did not prompt the decision, but simplicity — mine.

I hate confusion, and in the past ten years as a Christian I have made friends among every denomination imaginable (and unimaginable). Also I have a nodding acquaintance with members of minor groups within and without the approved bodies. Had I listened only to the teaching of each, I would have been changing denominations every six months or so.

As I have gone on with the one teacher, He has shown me that religion has *everything* to do with God and people getting together, and that His kind of religion is particularly for those who seem hardly at all religion-prone. It is exciting to discover for yourself that the Galilean had you in mind when He said, "Of such is the kingdom of heaven."

I wish to thank Gea, the other of the two ridiculous creatures, about whom you will shortly hear more, for her technical advice concerning our story. In answer to the question, "Do you feel that I was too rash when I said that we were ridiculous creatures?" (I was speaking from the couch; a writer's life is a hard one and I find I need to lie down often), she said, "What do you mean — *were?*" With this she sprang to her feet, spilling the sewing basket, stumbled over her shoes, danced neatly around three of her five children coloring on the floor (and I mean, floor), in time to throw the list of hymns she was to play on Sunday at her handsome minister-husband who was being dragged out of the door by their two horsey Doberman pinschers. I saw her pause long enough in the kitchen to give the spaghetti a stir and turn on the iron while helping Timmy pull off his boots, before she ran to pick up the screaming baby.

From the couch, I said with concern, "I didn't hear the baby crying!"

Every weekend or so I stop by at Gea and Wayne's house for small doses of tender domesticity to help keep me in touch with how the other half lives, and to get material for my newspaper column. Also I am indebted to Flicka and Greta, the dogs, who aided in shortening the manuscript by chewing up several chapters. I shall always love Lillabet, Jeremy, and Prisca, because they laughed and laughed when I told them about their mother and all the shoes she brought with her when we went to Switzerland — which greatly helped to give me the spirit of bravado necessary to write a book, any book, and particularly, a religious book.

CHAPTER XV

The Conductor Told Me

G ea had already slipped off her high heels, applied fresh make-up, run a comb through her shining black-brown hair, tucked her feet under her and was making herself comfortable on the wooden bench; that is, as comfortable as one can get in a third-class compartment of a Swiss train, while I was talking to the conductor in what I hoped was French.

I wasn't at all sure what he said, but I never let on to Gea. Traveling was the only area of living where I had had more experience than she, and I always treated her as if she were slightly demented the moment we'd get in motion.

"Don't get too relaxed," I warned, as I saw her crumpling up my tweed coat into a pillow. I continued, "The conductor told me that the Milano Express, *which we're on,* only makes a brief stop at Aigle, *where we're getting off,* and you must be ready at the exit to jump off the train, so I can throw our luggage to you from the window, then bolt for the door myself."

Gea took the news well. By this time she, too, had been traveling in Europe long enough to learn that they do things a little differently from the way we do in the States. Audibly I groaned while surveying the luggage strewn around us. I used to be a one-suitcase traveler before I met Gea.

"Hope *I* make it off the train," I muttered, "or I'll land at the Italian border."

I continued staring at the luggage.

"Don't come with that business about *my* shoes," she sniffed, flipping open a page of my mind dwelling on her shoes. "I'm sick of you always bringing up *my* shoes."

Not one to mince matters, she pointed to my tennis racquet,

golf clubs, three or four odd-shaped bags, mostly full of books and old magazines. "Books are a lot heavier than shoes," she let fly at me, "and furthermore, I only brought along a few pair this trip."

"Yeah, a few, like ten or twelve," I said, beginning to get a feeling for this skirmish.

Ignoring my comment, she said, "I can't see why you don't take up knitting, or collecting stamps — they're nice and light, but, *oh no,* books, books, wherever we go, we're dragging along *your* books." Suddenly she became bored with the argument, and said, "You might as well hand me one. For some strange reason I feel like reading."

I opened up one of the canvas bags, dug around and came up with a Bible. For fun I handed it to her.

"You're full of jokes today," she said sarcastically. "Here we are, on our way to the mountains, for the best time of our lives, and you drag along a Bible." She went on in a sing-song voice, "The course is over, we passed the exam, put the textbook away."

I dropped the Bible back into the sack and found a Sherlock Holmes story. "Better, that's better," and she even managed a smile.

Gea and I had met about a year before at Camp Eleanor on Lake Geneva, Wisconsin, where she was the music director, and I was the swimming and tennis instructor. I don't recall when we first talked about Switzerland, perhaps I always talked about it; but I believe that I was trying to explain to her why I was going back. It got involved, because it sounded melodramatic to say that there was an outer force compelling me to go back.

I embroidered a glamorous picture of Switzerland for her, not that Switzerland needs embellishing, but I tried to mention the things that would attract Gea. Fairly soon she, too, became enchanted with the thought of seeing Switzerland; but she left me with the uneasy sensation that she preferred that Switzerland come to her. Gea disliked traveling. Even coming from Kansas to Wisconsin had been a hardship for her. But I gargled on about how marvelous it was, what extraordinaire piano, drama, and ballet teachers there were in Lausanne. I was at the height of my persuasive power, having just talked my practical, sound father into seeing me through *one more year* of Switzerland. The approach I was using with my parents was that this added year was imperative to my career. In reality, this was quite a joke, as my "career" was as changeable as Gea's mind about young men. I had cooled off about being a writer. I didn't have anything to say, and I couldn't write about myself: I didn't know who I was.

One of the chief reasons Gea was hesitant about going to Switzerland was a boy friend back in Kansas.

I told her, "Gea, this is no problem. If the romance is real, Peter (Hastings, Tom, or whatever his name is) will be waiting at the dock when we return."

(I believe that it was around Christmas when he wrote that he was getting married; but, by this time, runner-up Gea was in full swing in the cultural life of Lausanne, and a lost boy friend in Kansas only caused her to leap higher in the ballet. And then it gave me the opportunity to say, "It must not have been the real thing." I do enjoy rounding out things, don't you?)

As Gea sat reading — by this time she had maneuvered the luggage, my tweed coat, and suede jacket to make herself really comfortable, I stared out the train window. I was thinking about the lecture series on the Bible we had attended in Lausanne, a few months before receiving this invitation to visit friends of Madame Dumreicher in the mountains. Gea too had set convictions about religion. She thought religion fine — for other people. She had tried in her younger days to find out about God, even to the extent of attending three or four confirmation classes; but the teaching was not too different from what she heard in her psychology and sociology courses at the university, so she gave up. But, like me, every once in awhile she was willing to try again, so when we read in the paper that a series of Bible lectures were to be given at the Scottish Church, in English and free, we decided to attend.

They were fairly interesting, and we did all the suggested reading, but when the course was over, the Bible went back on the shelf behind a large vase. The reason I had a Bible with me on this excursion was a quirk of mine. One of my grandmothers had given it to me years ago, and I always carried it with me wherever I went.

As we sped past the green vineyards along Lake Geneva, so neatly and carefully cultivated by the Swiss who live in the picturesque villages built into the hills, I started wondering about the people we were going to visit. Through Madame Dumreicher I had already met a delightful array of interesting people. There was the Danish couple who served champagne instead of coffee in the morning, the relative who edited the exclusive magazine which circulated in . . . . For all the world, it sounded as if the conductor had shouted, "Aigle!" where we were supposed to get off; but he stuck his head in at the far end of the coach only long enough to announce the stop, and immediately disappeared.

I catapulted into action, scaring Gea half to death. She had dozed off. This was one of the times when I wished the European conductors were like our American ones who hover about; but I did not say it, because one of the lectures I delivered frequently to Gea was, "Stay home if you're not willing to adjust."

We started adjusting all over the place. The train was already slowing down. The Swiss and their efficiency! They can bring these long trains to a stop before you can say, "Frère Jacques." I took a quick look out the window and spotted the depot sign. It *was* Aigle, unfortunately.

Gea was struggling to come awake and groping for her shoes. Immediately I sized up the situation. We'd have to change roles. I shouted to her that I was getting off first and that *she* would have to throw out our luggage. I bolted down the aisle and was at the exit door just as the train lurched to a halt.

I jumped off the step and ran along the side of the train to our compartment, prepared to catch the baggage. But no Gea. Suddenly a man raised the window and began to explain in French that the Mademoiselle was under the seat searching for her "slippers," but that he would be glad to start passing out our luggage. As I started to reach up for one of the suitcases, Gea appeared and started throwing out things. I yelled at her to make a break for the exit, but she was so engrossed in sailing out my books, my golf clubs, my tennis racquet, that she never heard me, and off she went to the Italian border as the train noiselessly glided away from the platform. The man who had tried to help us waved pleasantly before he closed the window.

CHAPTER XVI

We Come Alive

S witzerland is a small country. Gea went to the Italian border, got off, and stepped on to the waiting Paris express which came back through Aigle. She was the first and only person off at Aigle. I'm sure it wasn't a scheduled stop, but some people have a way even with train engineers. Actually I was relieved when I saw her, but I never gave her the satisfaction of knowing I was. When she sauntered over to the bench where I was sitting reading the Paris *Herald Tribune,* all I said was, "Oh, it's you."

As the train pulled out, Gea turned to wave to the conductor, brakeman, engineer and several others, all bowing, tipping hats, and smiling broadly.

"I see your little detour was not too arduous."

"Not too," she said coyly, and then added respectfully, "but as *you* said, the trains in Switzerland don't stop long."

As she seemed in a cheerful, humble mood, I decided against bawling her out. Furthermore, I had learned in the station that I had read the schedule wrong, and we still had another hour before our next train.

She asked, "Where's the luggage?"

"What's left of it, I've piled up by some milk cans that are to be loaded on the train to Monthey. Come on, let's go on the other side of the station, where there's a nice tearoom. We can have a bite of lunch. . . ." I cleared my throat and explained casually that we still had a little wait for the Monthey train. Wisely she said nothing.

We walked across a few tracks which are for the mountain trains to Leysin, Les Diablerets and Monthey-Champéry. It was a clear, warm day, and it felt great to be doing what we were doing, leisurely looking around. Aigle is a small, pleasant, prosperous town in the Rhone Valley, surrounded by vineyards, fruit trees, geraniums and mountains. Right from the station we had an outstanding view of Les Dents du Midi, the mountain range of seven peaks, found in the background of the many famous paintings of the Castle of Chillon on Lake Geneva.

While we were having tea, crescent rolls, three kinds of jam and jelly, butter and cheese, a small, red train backed in next to the terraced part of the tearoom where we were sitting. It was the train to Monthey. Where else but in Switzerland can you sit on the edge of a train yard and find it not only charming, but clean? We were separated from the train by a hedge and several large pots of red geraniums.

"I think they have hundreds of geranium inspectors in Switzerland," Gea commented, "whose only job is to see that every Swiss citizen is growing his quota of geraniums."

"They've done a commendable job here," I agreed. Everywhere we looked we could see the lifting touch of red, sometimes pink and white, or pink and red, but mostly all red. As we sat there, we started to rehash the series of events that had occurred to us since arriving in Switzerland back in September. . . .

Gea and I spent our first month in Lausanne in a dark, damp, cheap, and cheerless pension. It rained every day, and our high-ceiling, dimly lighted room was so cold we could see our breath when we talked to one another. The Swiss, having lived without coal during World War II, learned that it is possible to survive with a minimum of heat; and then, too, it has a lot to do with the knit underwear they all wear. We were miserable. Even I nearly forgot my love for Switzerland. Gea let me know twenty or thirty times a day that she wished she had never come; and I let her know thirty or forty times that I wished she had married Hastings or Cyril or whoever he was.

Then we got a break. It thawed us out tremendously. My professor of diction at the Conservatory told me that a friend of hers wanted to sublease her apartment immediatement. "You will love it," she exclaimed. "It is the most overheated apartment building in Lausanne, and not only that, my friend is an artist. Her place is charming. Come along, we'll go see it."

We picked up Gea, who was practicing the piano in one of the practice rooms, and walked over. As I have said, Lausanne is situated on seven levels, so you are either going up or down, which might help to explain part of Gea's distress the first month in Switzerland. I had insisted we get out and walk every day, even in the rain. With her high heels and Kansas background, the poor girl was in an enfeebled condition.

"The only disadvantage is these stairs," Mademoiselle Daulte puffed as we reached the fifth floor. We were somewhat behind her, as I was pushing Gea up the last flight. But, happily, the stairs proved to be the only disadvantage. We fell in love with our home away from home the moment the door was opened to us. I never did count all the paintings and etchings in the living room alone. It was the sort of warm room you walk into hoping the people who live there are going to ask you to stay for tea.

At the far end of the room there was a marble-topped fireplace, and we always had a fire. It wasn't needed for warmth. The apartment was, as Mademoiselle Daulte said, "overheated" according to Swiss standards; but, to our frozen American bones, it was just right, and with the extra glow on the hearth, we came alive.

Gea came alive the day we moved in. A little too alive. One night she was propped up on the settee by the fireplace, and I was lying on the floor reading. I had my feet on a hassock (good for circulation), and my head on a few pillows (terrible for posture), when I began to get an uneasy sensation that I was being stared at. Gea was sitting there doing nothing but examining me as if I were a odd piece of sculpture in a modern art museum.

"What are you doing?" I blurted out. "Am I on fire or something?" I was lying close to the open fireplace.

"Be quiet, and turn your head to the right," she ordered in a tone I was beginning to recognize as trouble. For me. "To the right, not the left," she barked. "Now smile."

"Smile!" I snarled. "Cut this out, idiote." I turned my back on her, and added lamely, "You're so silly."

Completely ignoring me, she announced with an air of satisfaction, "Well, I believe I can do *something* with you. Now that I've had time to study you, it's not quite as hopeless as I first thought. There are a few areas worth cultivating."

By this time I was on my feet raving, "What are you talking about?"

93

She then explained calmly how shocked she had been when she first met me. The director of the camp in Wisconsin, who was also from Kansas, had told Gea about the other members of the staff, and the one who sounded interesting to her was the "world traveler" (me). She said icily, "Naturally I was expecting to meet a smart looking, fascinating person, but *you!*" She seemed to have run out of words, but only for a moment. "You," she said, *"you* have less feeling for clothes than our egg lady!" She clapped her hand against her forehead, "And your *shoes!* Oh! I detest those walking shoes you wear for best, and to think you had the nerve to bring along that other dreadful pair!"

She was referring to a pair of white loafers I wore at camp which were always parked at the entrance to the pier when I was on life guard duty. They had been through a lot, true, but were still grand, comfortable shoes. This was not our first (nor last) discussion about shoes.

When we were packing to go to Switzerland, there seemed to be nothing but shoes in the room. All Gea's. Green shoes, purple shoes, toeless shoes, silver dancing slippers, high heels, higher heels and Alpine heels. . . . I kept explaining to her that when you travel by air, you must be selective about what you take along. She finally saw it my way and brought along only a few of her favorite shoes, about nineteen or twenty pairs.

I hadn't really bothered much about my appearance (or shoes) until Gea presented the unvarnished facts about my dumpiness. If I had any goal about clothes and shoes, it can be said in five words. I like to be comfortable.

To divert Gea's attention I read her a portion from the psychology book I had in my hand. The author was showing, using a number of vivid illustrations, that it is generally the middle child in a family who is the problem. After I read the page, I asked casually, "Let's see, you do have an older and younger sister?" I never remember statistics, but I love to hear them.

She answered politely in the affirmative and seemed deeply interested in what I had just read to her; but then she added, as abruptly as she got up from the settee, "And may I call to your attention that you have an older brother, a younger brother and sister!" As she stepped over me, snapping shut my book, she announced, "And now, middle daughter, *come with me!* We are going to inspect your wardrobe."

I was planning to go to bed anyway, so after a short interval, I strolled carelessly into the bedroom. Already she had my two tweed suits thrown upon the bed (my good clothes) and slacks, blouses, and jackets strewn around; and, as I entered the room, I caught her dropping into the waste basket my good walking shoes!

"Aha!" I said with authority, "this is going too far!" I ordered her out of the room. I might as well have been talking to the statue of William Tell down on the corner. She was engrossed in examining one of my suits. "As I suspected," she said in disgust, "size twenty."

She eyed me critically, "It wouldn't surprise me if you are a size sixteen; with some work, possibly fourteen!"

She stepped over and before I could protect myself, she punched me hard in the middle, "Thick here, but other than that, a fairly decent figure, that is, if you knew how to walk and sit." She sat down on the bed, sighed deeply, and said, "Whew, we have a lot to do, Alpine Annie, but we're doing it. I can't stand unfinished products."

The "improvement program" began that night. First she went to work on my hair. It was bleached out by the sun, blown apart by the wind on the many bicycle trips I had made, and looked like a miniature haystack on top of my head; at least, that is what the fairy godmother said. Then possibly the fact that it had been cut, singed, chopped, and permanented in twelve or thirteen countries in the past five years had not done much for it.

At first I was furious about all the nonsense she put me through and sabotaged her every opportunity I got. But one day we went shopping. She picked out a handsome, size fourteen, blue and white checked suit. While trying it on, I stole a few glances in the mirror and couldn't quite believe it. I had been on a rigorous diet for several weeks, and those exercises she put me through! Worse than anything in the WAVES. No wonder I was trimmer.

Then my hair began to come alive. As part of the regime, she brushed my hair every night for one hundred or seven hundred strokes and worked in a lanolin preparation. I went around the apartment smelling like a goat, but it worked wonders. Even I had to admit that for years my hair had been the color and texture of seaweed after it has been lying on the beach a few days. You would have thought Gea had discovered uranium the night she detected a flash of honey-colored hair. Also there were the various creams that she slapped on my face, tedious walks about the apartment with a book on my head, a course in applying make-up, and then, of course, shoes.

Next we shopped for shoes. It was exhausting to shop with the expert. She never bought until she had compared the merchandise in every store in town. Up and down the rue de Bourg we trudged, in and out of Innovation, big shoe stores and little ones. My system in shopping was to run into the nearest shop, buy the first thing, and race out. At first I was adamant when she had a clerk show me high heels with straps in the back. "You mean I'm supposed to *walk* in those?" I asked in genuine amazement.

She and the patient clerk insisted I try, at least. I never gave them the satisfaction of knowing, but the shoes were very comfortable, nearly as easy to walk in as my walking shoes.

One evening a couple of months after the "improvement program" got under way, we were again sitting in the living room, this time Gea on the floor, and me, upright on the settee. We had just returned from a concert. During the intermission I was standing with a couple of fellows from the Conservatory at the coffee bar. Gea had gone into the lounge. While she was there, two ladies came in, and one said to the other, "Did you see that woman at the coffee bar? For a moment I thought it was Ingrid Bergman!"

The rest of the night the fairy godmother was ecstatic. She kept whispering, "See, what did I tell you!"

There happened to be ten or twelve other women standing around the bar, but Gea to this day insists they were talking about her "prodigy." I had no way of knowing, because during the entire "improvement" era, I was forbidden to wear my glasses, except for reading; and, being extremely near-sighted, I probably was standing next to the famous movie star. I'll never know.

The days of glamor lasted about three months, and then we both got so busy with other things, Gea relaxed on me; and I drifted comfortably into a middle-of-the-road position, neither Alpine Annie nor Enchanting Ingrid, but something vastly improved from the days of walking shoes and size twenty tweeds.

Gea worked hard on the piano the first few months in Switzerland, that is, when she wasn't improving me. But then she started taking ballet lessons, and gradually "the dance" began to be her life. Everything was "the dance," and for a spell she hardly touched the piano. That gave me a break. I was still taking lessons at the Conservatory, so I felt that I should do some practicing at home. But I never dared to play when Gea was around. I respected her sensitive ear, and after a while, I began to respect mine, and gave up the piano. I had quite enough to do with my other courses in psychology, poetry, and French literature.

Then there was the marketing. It takes time in Switzerland, but it's delightful.

CHAPTER XVII

"To Market"

To market in Lausanne you must start early in the morning with a large basket and several folded string bags in your pocket, in case the purchases should spill over. And they always did. At the top of the rue de Bourg, a narrow, cobblestoned street up from the Place St. François in the heart of the city, is the best place to begin. The buildings are old, quaint, but beautifully kept up, and painted in pastel colors with large window boxes bursting with red geraniums. Also on the diminutive street are several fashionable shops, a couple of bookstores and record shops where I spent hours, more than one tearoom, a well-known toy shop, an important furrier, and miscellaneous stores.

On both sides of the narrow street the stands with their colorful wares are set up. Every Wednesday and Saturday morning, the year round, is market day in Lausanne, and the people from around the countryside pour in. If you were going into one of the dress shops, first you have to step through a garden of onions, carrots, cabbages, squash, hanging sausages, large rounds of cheese, and large baskets of flowers.

There are blocks and blocks of market, down the steep hill, past Innovation, Lausanne's second largest department store, where they introduced popcorn to the Swiss the year Gea and I were there. And the market winds on around the historic City Hall, past a fountain in the court, and on to the main market place. Here you can buy anything from home-baked bread to men's trousers.

I loved marketing in Lausanne. It looked good, smelled good, it was good. I stopped to chat with the rosy-cheeked lady who counted out a dozen eggs for me. "Very 'fraiches,'" she assured me. I never knew exactly what flowers to get, so I ended up doing what

I always did, bought several bunches, then an armful at another stand. Nearby I visited with a smiling farm lady who always sold us homemade bread and anise cookies. She asked in French, "Where is the lovely young lady?"

Gea and I usually went to market together, but she had recently become interested in an art class at the University, and had gone to register.

There were many vegetables and fruits from which to choose, but I stuck to the ones I knew and could pronounce. I wandered for hours.

Later in the day, I went out again to the meat market. You could buy meat at the outdoor market, but we had a favorite store down the street from us, where a couple of the younger clerks enjoyed teasing us about our French. Also I made the other rounds. The supermarket had not invaded Switzerland as yet, and so I went to the "laiterie" for milk, the droguerie for hand cream, the pharmacie for aspirin, and to the tobacco shop for a newspaper. There is no slipping into these small shops, making a quick purchase, and hurrying out. As you enter you are greeted with a cordial, "Bonjour, Mademoiselle," and an inquiry as to your health. Then follows much smiling, nodding, and exclaiming. After the few purchases are made, the proprietor often walks with you to the door, holds it open, bows, and says, "Au revoir, Mademoiselle."

That afternoon after I had finished the marketing, I decided to walk down to Ouchy. It is all down hill to get there, as Ouchy is the port of Lausanne, and my favorite spot in Switzerland. The Swiss in their thoroughness and amazing sense of neatness, beauty, and what's right, have placed a public park on the edge of the lake. There are blocks of wide, comfortable walking paths bordered with flowers according to the season. Every few feet there is another bed of flowers more colorful and imaginatively arranged than the one just passed. If Ouchy had only flowers, it would be worth seeing, but that is only part of the picture. Because of the hills around Lausanne, Ouchy (pronounced, OO-she, not Ouch-ee) is sheltered from the glacial air that blows off the Alps, and the year-round temperature is moderate; so the vegetation is more lush than you'd expect north of Italy. In the park are stately trees, many flowering trees, and a variety of unusual smaller trees and shrubs.

A stone wall separates the lake from the pathway, high enough to sit on if you desire, and now and then the wall juts around a group of weeping willows. Also there are benches all along the path, and as if all this were not enough, across the glorious carpet of blue-green lake loom the violet-edged Savoy Alps in France.

After I had fed the swan and watched a white steamer come into the quai, I walked past the Beau Rivage Hotel where guests were having afternoon tea, and went and sat on a bench close to the Chateau d'Ouchy. I thought of the many times Madame Dumreicher and I had strolled along the promenade and stopped at the Chateau. I smiled at the remembrance of the waiters fluttering around my friend. A tap of her cane, that charm of hers, and we had more service than we knew what to do with. But the tea parties in her room at the pension of cats and old people were even better. If she wasn't feeling well, she'd direct me to the needed utensils. Sometimes I'd find the electric water heater back in the closet under shoes, and it would be another adventure locating the cord. Once I found the teapot in a large box of old photos. She put her arms around the box after I had extracted the pot. "Here are all my beloved people," said she, and tea would be postponed as we looked at the precious faces of family and friends scattered over the world, and many who had died tragically. She would shed a few tears, and then abruptly the box was closed and the cheerful tea party began. Having a hot plate and serving food in your room was strictly forbidden, and it always brightened up the Baroness to reign at these secret parties. The last summer when I was in the States, and before she moved to England, she went to the mountains for a holiday. When she came back, she was terribly excited about a family she had met in Champéry. "I cannot be explaining," she tried to tell me, "but these peoples you must be meeting someday."

But Gea and I were so involved in Lausanne, we never had time to go to Champéry. . . . GEA! I came out of my dream world abruptly, and ran for the bus. This was the ballet night. Gea wanted to eat early, and I was the cook of the week.

CHAPTER XVIII

The Duck Ballet

I had the salad halfway made and some rolls in the oven when Gea came in. The minute she whirled into the apartment, I thought — I shouldn't have done it, I shouldn't have done it. She greeted me with an arabesque and a cheerful, "Hi!"

As she waltzed toward the bedroom, she was chanting, "There is nothing like 'the dance,' 'the dance,' 'the dance. . . .'"

I was in the kitchen, putting the finishing touches on the supper, but I could hear her frantically going through the closet. Then in a flash, she was at the kitchen door. She must have made a "grand jeté," a very *big* leap. She demanded, "Where is my pink tutu?"

"Where is your *what?*" I tried playing innocent.

"You know," she hurled at me, splintering my innocence, "my tutu's" — all of them." She fixed her eye upon me.

I busied myself finishing the salad, ignoring her and trying to avoid "the eye." I was attempting to place a red cherry in the center of some melon balls. She moved directly in front of me, blue eyes blazing.

"What did you do with them?"

"Oh, Gea, all right!" If I hadn't worked so hard getting the cherry in the center of the fruit, I would have shoved it in her face. I added, rather calmly, "I put them in the basement — *all* of them. Even the pink one!"

Less calmly, I continued, "Every time I go into the closet I get scratched or hit in the eye by one of those blasted skirts. They stick out a mile, and furthermore, to be honest, I thought once you got started with the art course, you'd be through with the ballet."

Me and my "furthermore's."

She glowered at me,

"Me, through with *the ballet! ! ! !"*

I began to wonder how I could have thought such a thing.

"OK, OK, Pavlova, I'm convinced," I said sarcastically. "The dance goes on." Wearily I added, "I'll go get them *right now."*

Mostly I was mad at myself. I had acted hastily, foolishly; and I was also mad, because when I carried all those costumes into the basement, I meant for them to stay there. How do you win with these loud, stubborn creatures?

However, she was not heartless. She made the second trip with me. Seventy-five steps to the ground level, and another twelve to the basement. And up again.

At supper we were cool toward one another over the melon balls. Then I started to get that uncomfortable feeling. Oh no, I thought miserably, she's hatching *another* idea. She led off rather formally,

"My dear Miss Carlson, I find it tragic that you are so out of sympathy with dancing. You have learned through our association by now that I am a true friend, because I take an interest in your *total* welfare."

It was the way she hit *total* that unnerved me. But I thought craftily to myself, I'll just pretend to go along with her, whatever she's stirring up this time, and at the right moment, I can kid her out if it; and so I said graciously, but cautiously,

"Thank you, dear friend."

She ignored me and went straight to the point.

"I have decided that you are going with me tonight to the dance class," she said firmly.

I attempted a few polite, small laughs, choking badly on a piece of cantaloupe; but I realized with a half-strangled feeling that I'd have to break both ankles and my neck to maneuver out of the web being spun.

She rocked back in the needlepoint chair, eyes glittering. "Yes, of course, I'm surprised that I didn't think of this before. This *is* the solution. You are going with me." She added with condescension and pity, "You know nothing about 'the dance' — how *could* you love it?"

"All right, Gea," I said pleasantly, "I'll go with you tonight." Then I said casually, sort of looking out the window, "It'll undoubtedly do me a lot of good to watch."

"Oh, darling," she said with a light, witchy laugh, "You're not going to watch. You're going to dance!"

With that she pushed herself away from the table and floated dreamily around the room.

"You're going to love to dance!"

It was a dreadful thought to me, dreadful. The "improvement program" was bad enough, but at least it didn't involve other people in the initial stages; but the thought of going into a ballet class. . . . I don't have a ballet bone in my body, not one. A novelist describing a certain character could say, "Well built, reserved, and stiff." That's me. I enjoy watching others dance, great emphasis on others; and of all forms of dancing, the ballet was the one I was least likely to move around in inconspicuously. I like swimming, tennis, squash, where rhythm and motion are vital, but dancing? No Ma'am, not for me. And the ballet? Ach! Alors! Never, *never*. How ridiculous can some people get?

I announced with finality, this was too big a matter to kid about.

"Gea, this is one thing you're not talking me into. You've had your little joke, now run along. Me, dance! Utter nonsense! Childish babbling!"

My voice must have come out stronger than I meant, because the dishes in the cabinet behind me were rattling, and one crashed to the floor when I added, *"Jamais de ma vie!"*

I wasn't sure what it meant, but it thoroughly intimidated Gea. I snatched the dishes from the table and in stony silence cleaned up the kitchen.

To this day I do not know *how* she did it. She must have drugged me, but twenty minutes later I waddled from the bedroom to the living room in Gea's yellow "tutu," long black stockings and ballet slippers. All I could possibly say was, "Quack."

"Quack, quack."

Never have I felt more like a duck. Something about those toe shoes made my feet turn out; and the costume, having been carried up and down the stairs twice that day, was badly out of shape and stuck out in back.

I kept repeating, "Quack, quack."

Gea came lightly from the bedroom in her pink "tutu." "Why in the world," she asked, "are you making that ridiculous sound?"

"I feel like a duck."

She gave me a strange look, but said with enthusiasm, "You look great!"

What an actress, that woman! What a liar.

Then she became all business.

"To brief you quickly for this evening, we'll try the five positions." Briskly she said, "Step to the 'barre,' please."

"Good," I chirped, "I sure can use a drink!"

My attempt at humor was as out of place as a few cheers at a funeral. Gea was playing the role of dance professor now, and there was no retreating.

She explained, "The 'barre' in ballet is a long, fairly pliable wooden rod attached to the wall a bit above waist height. The basic ballet steps are practiced at the 'barre.' Obviously, we do not have a 'barre' — so let's use the back of this chair."

She shoved a chair over to me.

The lesson continued for an hour, and by the end of that time I knew the positions. At least, in my mind — "Heels together, toes out," etc., etc.; but my legs, arms, and torso never got the message. Gea was exhausted, but not defeated. She adored adversity and challenge. I was a total wreck.

She looked at the clock. "We have to run," she said. "The class starts in a few minutes."

We changed to jeans and plaid shirts and "pirouetted" out the door. That is, Gea did. I followed sullenly. As we walked quickly along, I asked anxiously,

"What are you going to tell the professor?"

"Oh, I'll just tell him you want to try out. Don't let him frighten you. It's only artistic temperament."

"What's his name?"

"I can't pronounce it. We call him Monsieur Tutu."

We moved noiselessly down the rue de Bourg, across the Place St. François, past the Cathedral, waved at the white-gloved gendarme who was directing the light flow of traffic from his special box at the end of the square, and ran on across the high Roman bridge and soon were at the auditorium.

We rushed directly to the ladies' dressing room. There was a charged, excited atmosphere in the small room. It looked like a Degas painting with women in different stages of dress and colorful "tutu's" hanging all over. I was nearly kicked in the face as I passed too close to a dancer doing a foot-and-leg exercise.

Everybody knew Gea. The "bonjour's" were flying. I was introduced to a few friends, but we had little opportunity to talk, as everyone was hurrying to get into her costume. As I started pulling on mine, I had to discipline myself to keep the "quacks" from coming out again. Then I had an awful time lacing my slippers. The tutu nearly strangled me. Gea is a good size and a half smaller than I, and inches shorter. I had difficulty bending over. She came over and laced me up, attempted to flatten the part of my tutu that stuck out in the back, gave up. As we started for the door, she again assured me I looked "great," and out we went. Gea with a graceful leap. Me, waddling.

I was presented to the "Maître de Danse," who to my surprise was a short, stout man, past his prime in the theater; but once the class got going I saw why he was the teacher, and why his class was popular. He lived "the dance." His heart, soul, and short, stout body were in every gesture. As Gea had told me earlier in the evening, "To make the ballet live, it must be made to materialize in the flesh and blood of the dancers."

Monsieur Tutu was doing exactly that, and he drew it out of his pupils, all but the one who was told to take her position directly behind Gea (commonly known as, me). I didn't dare dwell on what the professor must have thought when he saw me, but soon I had so much on my mind, I forgot all about him.

"As soon as the music begins," Gea hissed, "simply do everything I do. The first record is a little warm-up drill."

A "little warm-up drill," she said. I'll bet the Marines don't work as hard. It started out fairly modestly, arms swaying to the left and right, and ethereal expressions on the faces of the ballet corps. Suddenly, in the midst of the palm tree swaying, the tempo of the music abruptly changed, and we started to do knee bends, "plié," they are called in French. The first time around we did only a few, and then the music picked up tempo, and we began "plee-aye-ing" like crazy. Soon my knees felt stretched beyond any hope of normal recovery, my head was spinning from bending over, straightening up, bending over (my brains hadn't undergone such violence since that time I fell out of a hayloft and landed on my head).

Desperately I slipped in a few modified "plee-ayes," bending slightly and keeping my knees straight.

Above the music and creaking of joints Monsieur Tutu screamed, "Non, non, non, Mademoiselle!" and his stick was pointing directly at me, "Plee-aye, plee-aye, plee-aye! ! !"

It scared me sufficiently so the adrenalin started pouring into the muscles around my knees, and I dipped to the ground a few more times, but I was beginning to ache all over.

Suddenly the music changed again, and everybody moved forward in tiny, short steps on their toes. About the time I got momentum to get up on my toes, I met the class tiptoeing back again. Gea whispered as she spun me around (happily the professor was bawling out some one else and didn't see me),

"This is the 'pas de bourrée'."

As if that meant anything to me, but as I was clumping along, now going with the group, instead of against, it came to me. Aha! I thought, the "pas de boo-ray" — she had explained it in the private lesson. This is the dainty step used in romantic and classical ballet to give the illusion of floating. Some in the class, like Gea, were actually doing it, but I was happy to observe that a number were thrashing about, and a few, like myself, had sunk.

This "little warm-up exercise" was followed by a brief interval of soothing music, when we all rose up slowly on our toes and made little bows with our hands above our heads while revolving clockwise. I didn't notice until the "Maître de Danse" screeched it to my attention, but I was going counter.

While this maneuver was going on, I stole a few glances around me. There were easily fifty people in the room, and a mixed crowd if ever I saw one. Gea had previously explained that it was a unique class. She wasn't kidding. All sizes, shapes, ages, and a few men — boys, I should say. This was ballet for the proletarian and bourgeoisie, an unusual thing in Europe where there is still class distinction.

I had an odd sensation when I looked at two dancers in particular. They looked very familiar, but in those costumes and the ethereal expressions on their faces, I doubt if I would have recognized my own mother had she slipped into the class. I tried frantically to place them in my mind. The one who bothered me the most was the chap next to me. I knew I knew him. On his next revolving I got a good look at him. I nearly fell off my toes. It was one of our butchers. Then immediately it registered: the lady next to him was the one I bought peanuts from in the Grand Magasin, Lausanne's "dime store." Also in the class were a number of students, like Gea, who had found out that Monsieur Tutu was the best and cheapest ballet teacher in Lausanne.

They all had one thing in common — the meatman, the clerk, the students, and their professor — they loved to dance. Every small gesture was made with deep feeling. I only wished that I had had a built-in camera that evening. Even I was beginning to enjoy it, but the pleasant stretching exercise (the only one I was able to do) came to an abrupt halt.

I had hardly rocked back on my heels when the wild horse music began. Gea grabbed me and yanked me in beside herself and next to the butcher. I'd give anything to know what it was that was played for this part of the drill. Ever so often it comes stampeding across my mind, and I'm transported back to the night in Switzerland when I danced the ballet.

At a certain signal we were off! I never got the signal. The butcher sure did. With a magnificent spraying of legs and arms, he nearly mowed me down, as he thrust himself into his first "grand jeté" of the evening. I don't believe he saw me. I know he didn't. That lad was in another world, and it surely was not the world of sausages, pork chops, and lamb patties. And so were all the others — in another world, a wonderful world of carefree leaping, hilarious jumping, glorious gamboling.

The air was charged with gleeful dancers making great leaps. I figured out after awhile, as I dodged this one and that one, that in reality they were all leaping in a circle; but what made for confusion and danger was that some out-leaped others. Legs were flying on all sides of me. I watched for an opening, and finally edged myself into a safe corner, where I could try a few modest leaps myself without being trampled to death.

There was something about that wild horse music that brought out the leap in a man. Someday, somewhere, in a concert hall, I know I shall hear *that* music again. What pandemonium will follow! I delight in thinking about it.

Just when I was getting ready to make a timid hop into the air myself, the butcher was upon me again, and to keep from being squashed, I gave with a splendid "grand jeté" to the left. The best leap of my life, but too much for Gea's costume. It split right down the middle, and I streaked to the ladies' dressing room.

I wasn't missed. Even Monsieur Tutu was springing around the auditorium. And soon after, the class was involved in arabesques, with each member of the corps de ballet concentrating on perfecting the most trifling detail of his or her technique.

I removed what was left of Gea's yellow "tutu," put on my jeans and plaid shirt, and slipped quietly to a bench in the rear part of the gymnasium and watched the remainder of the remarkable performance.

Thus began and ended my career as a ballerina. Gea never said another word about it. She too, shortly after this, grew weary of "the dance." In fact, we were getting weary of a lot of things we were doing. It unnerved us pretty badly to find out how bored and tired we really were.

CHAPTER XIX

Some Discoveries

Y ou cannot live on close terms with someone without discovering little things about that person which did not show up before. By the time we had moved into the overheated apartment, Gea had learned that I had black moods; and when I had one, it was not pleasant to be near me. I do not know if you have lived with a moody person. It isn't pleasant. And it is far from pleasant being *that person.*

I never knew exactly what was wrong; different things would trigger me off. Particularly when I was put into a position where I'd have to think soberly about what was the point in life; or like that time when Jean Paul asked me if I ever thought about death. I kept myself going most of the time by having fun, keeping busy so I wouldn't have to think; and finding interesting, stimulating friends to share adventures. But every once in awhile I'd completely lose my sense of humor, and when I did, I was lost.

I recall clearly one night when I was in a state of depression, Gea came bounding into the living room where I was sitting in the dark staring out the window. She was singing and greeted me cordially. I snarled back. It made her furious. Angrily she said,

"You've been drooping and growling around here for two days now. I came in as pleasantly and cheerfully as I know how. I simply give up, I don't know how to treat you when you're in one of your horrid *moods.*"

With that she ran into the bedroom and slammed the door. After a few seconds, I went out and slammed the hall door.

I walked for several miles, hard and fast. At first I wasn't conscious of anything, only the sense of wanting to get away. I slowed down my pace as I began to ponder what I was trying to get away from. Then a horrid thought struck me, most of all, I was trying to run from myself; and what a losing battle I was fighting! Then I began to have a sensation of being pursued, it wasn't a frightening feeling of being chased by a person; it was more of an overshadowing, an outside force pressing down. I had had the feeling before, but never as intense as this time.

Suddenly I found myself at the little park I had discovered my first day in Lausanne. I ran down the steps and slumped onto a bench. And there I sat and looked and tried not to think or feel. I could see the lights of Evian across the lake, like lightning bugs, which reminded me of summer evenings in Illinois; and, as I was watching, the moon came from behind clouds and paved a path of silver and gold upon the lake.

I whispered, "God?"

It was only a question, but then I spoke His name again, and a feeble prayer arose from within me. It was a cry of despair, but I felt better having told someone that I was at my wits' end. Then I cried. That too felt good. I hadn't cried freely since I was a child; and so I cried some more; and then, after awhile, I walked slowly back to the apartment.

Gea was sitting on the settee reading. There was a fire in the fireplace, and she had dusted and straightened up the room, and rearranged several bouquets of flowers. It looked inviting and peaceful. As I stood by the door, I felt foolish and ashamed, yet my pride would not let me say, "Please forgive me." Desperately I wanted to communicate to Gea, but I had no idea how to get through to her. She continued reading, noisily flipped a page as I stood awkwardly saying nothing. The silence was dreadful. Finally I blurted out, "I know you can't stand to discuss religion, but shut up and listen!"

As soon as these words rolled from my tongue, I realized how ridiculous I sounded, and almost at the same time, we laughed. She listened earnestly as I tried to explain what had happened to me in the park, then she surprised me by saying, "I've been sitting here doing some thinking myself. We've really missed the boat some place along the line."

We talked far into the night and early morning; and then when one of us read the announcement in the paper about the Bible lectures, we decided to go.

"A little religion is good for anyone," I told Gea, as we walked to the Scottish Church. The lectures were fairly interesting, as I said earlier, but the slant the minister gave to the Bible reaffirmed our conviction that Christianity was a little religion and not broad enough for our questing minds and hungry hearts. When the course was over, the Bible was put away, and we again got busy having fun, running here, running there. Soon I forgot the desperation of that night in the park, the serious talk with Gea and our confessing to each other that we knew something serious was missing in our lives.

Around this time I discovered that I really did want to be a writer and that the best thing for a writer to do is to write. Writers had always greatly impressed Gea, so she tiptoed around me whenever the typewriter was out on the dining room table, and did nearly all of her practicing at the Conservatory. She was back to studying the piano.

CHAPTER XX

The Deluge Begins

A great interest of mine in the winter and spring of 1951 was the thought of the many advantages which would occur if the Continent and England would forgive and forget their many grievances with one another and form a United States of Europe. You cannot live in Switzerland and not be impressed with the differences of the people living together in this one small country. In an area with the greatest distance east-west, 226 miles, and north-south, 137 miles, there are four official languages, four cultural backgrounds, four separate ways of life; and the Swiss French don't particularly like the Swiss Germans, and the Swiss Germans think *they're* frivolous, and so on and on. But the Swiss have seen the wisdom of standing together under one flag, with the result that they are not only at peace among themselves, but they have stood for over a hundred years with wars being fought on all sides of them, as a living symbol of peace.

Another person in the post-World War II era intrigued with the thought of uniting Europe was a certain Frenchman by the name of Charles DeGaulle. I read an article of his in a Paris newspaper and immediately wrote to him thanking him for the good article and encouraging him to persevere in the plan to unite Europe (would that he had!). A few days after I wrote, I received a cordial letter from Madame DeGaulle explaining that her husband was in North Africa and she'd have him write to me when he came back. And she did what she said. Not long after, I had a letter from the General himself. He wasn't as busy in those days as he has been recently. He thanked me for my letter and urged *me* to persevere with the idea of a United States of Europe.

I became more and more captivated with the thought, and

stayed awake nights thinking about what Europe could do if there were a common currency, common language, common trade agreements, and mutual standing together, so they'd have reasons to care for one another, rather than to kill each other. Then I also became interested in urging other American students to come to Europe to study and live for a while. Nearly everything I wrote in that period had something about "good will among men."

With the enthusiasm of Tom Paine, I mailed to the United States about fifty or sixty "good will" messages. One of these open letters to the young people in the States was printed in the *Miami Herald,* and a sailor stationed in Florida read the letter, and promptly wrote to me. He commended my fine spirit in wishing "good will among men," and then, supporting his argument with Bible verses, he endeavored to show me I had made a serious omission. His parting words were, "Without Christ, there is no good will among men."

You must have this clearly in mind — if there was a type of human being who really irritated me in those days, it was a person who quoted Scripture to prove anything. I had already categorized the Bible as a fine book, beautiful literature, but not "the" authority. But I was impressed to receive a fan letter, and wrote back to the sailor and thanked him for his letter. Then, feeling it my duty to help lift him out of his narrow-minded rut, I informed *him,* tactfully, of course, that his conclusions were pathetic, that none of the educated people in the enlightened twentieth century believed that Christ had anything to do with "good will among men." Very kindly, I suggested that he open a few other books and "get with it."

Within a week, he sent another letter. He matched my kindliness of tone, only he made it very, very plain that *I* was the one who was wrong, and he suggested that I read the Bible.

Our telling off one another went on for a spell. Then I wrote him a firm letter and spelled it out quite clearly that I thought he was a crackpot. When I mailed the letter, I said to Gea, "That's goodbye to my sailor, enough is enough."

She had been following our correspondence with interest. He had sent several pictures of himself, and I must say, as Gea said, "For a religious fanatic, he was very handsome."

But the boy wouldn't stay submerged. He had merely been clearing his throat in the first few letters. He began to write nearly every day. He must have been on light duty; just copying all those Bible verses took time.

Then the deluge began. We hadn't seen anything yet. He began to send booklets, tracts, magazines, articles on prayer, book markers (with Bible verses on both sides), and a variety of Christian books. The postage alone must have slimmed down his Seaman Third Class pay envelope; and it cost me something — I had to buy another bookcase.

I looked over everything he sent. A dreadful habit of mine, being so fascinated by the printed page, is that I cannot resist at least scanning material put into my hands. It became a joke between Gea and me, and at the same time, something to look forward to. "Well, what has our sailor sent today?" she would ask if I happened to be the one to walk down the five flights to pick up our mail.

Once the sailor came into our lives, things started to move fast. In fact, it was as if the wild horse music was being played. It got wild. I am not positive about the sequence of some of the next events; but the important thing is, this crazy chain of events all happened. And it happened wham, slam, bang.

1. We bought a motor scooter.
2. Gea found a beautiful lute in a second hand store.
3. We bought it.
4. I got a mandolin.
5. An idea started forming.
6. We were enamored with the thought of spreading good will in Europe.
7. Personally.
8. Among men.
9. And women.
10. We worked out a musical show to take on the road (the idea was as ancient as strolling troubadours, only we were going on a motor scooter; I knew Gea would never make it on foot).
11. We needed one more trouper in the act, so we wrote a convincing letter to a friend we had met at camp.
12. There was nothing in the way of acting, singing, playing instruments that Marianne could not do.
13. She came.
14. All the way from Chicago.

15. But the Marianne who arrived in Lausanne wasn't the same Marianne we had known. She came with a Bible.

    a. She read it every night.

    b. She tried to tell us about something "wonderful" that had happened to her.

    c. We thought, "Yeah, she's off her rocker,"

    d. Like the poor sailor.

16. What really perturbed us, when we told Marianne we were planning to entertain people, she said she didn't feel like entertaining people. Sadly she added, "You will have to find someone else."

17. We couldn't find someone else; and furthermore, we had written our skits and songs *around her*.

18. I developed a serious sinus infection.

    a. Very serious.

    b. Taken to hospital.

    c. Operated on.

        (1) It was a traumatic experience being operated on in a foreign language.

        (2) I was what is known in both English and French as "miserable."

19. While I was convalescing, Gea and Marianne ran the motor scooter into a taxi.

    a. Fortunately no one hurt, but all shook up.

    b. End of motor scooter.

20. End of dream to go "troubadouring."

21. To spread good will among men.

22. At the height (or depth) of our total misfortune, we met a Swiss friend, who said, "You look dreadful, both of you. What is the matter?" We enumerated the twenty-one points. "Well," she said cheerfully, "it is simple. When you need to get over something in Switzerland, you go to the mountains."

That night I said to Gea, "That's a wonderful idea, let's go to the mountains!"

"Great," she replied sarcastically. "Are we planning to print our own money?"

23. Ach, alors, zut. I forgot; no money. Lute, mandolin, motor scooter, operation, accident. We were broke.

24. The following morning, *the* letter arrived. It was from Madame Dumreicher in England. It started out, "I am just receiving

a letter from the Schaeffers in Champéry. They are demanding me, dear, if you are still in Switzerland, and why you are no visiting them. I only ask you, Schatzi, why you are not?"

I shouted, "Gea, Gea!"

She was in the kitchen — her week to cook. But it was no great problem: we were down to three cans of beans.

I shouted again, "We're on our way to the mountains!"

She came leaping.

She snatched the letter from me. As she read on, a wonderful smile covered her face. She had an unopened can of beans in her hand. She put it to her ear, like Madame Dumreicher's ear trumpet, and said, "I only ask you, Schatzi, why we are not?"

25. She did a few "grand jetés."

26. I sat down and wrote a letter.

27. To the Schaeffers in the Swiss Alps.

28. Almost immediately we received a reply (the Swiss postal system is one of the best in the world). Mrs. Schaeffer said they were looking forward to our coming *that* weekend and "we hope you will be able to remain with us at least a week or two. We have plenty of room. . . . Madame Dumreicher has told us many things about you, and we . . ." etc., etc.

29. In the same batch of mail was one of the Christian magazines sent by the sailor. I leafed through it.

30. I noticed a picture of an attractive woman at the head of a column. It started out differently than the usual literature the sailor sent, so I sat down and read it.

"Gea," I called. This time she was in the bedroom packing. Champéry is a well-known summer and winter resort, and Gea wanted to be sure she had clothes *and* shoes for every occasion, afternoon dancing at the hotel, parties in the evening, teas, candlelight dinners. For someone going to the mountains to recover from an accident, she seemed pretty revived already, I thought.

"Listen to this." I read the first paragraph from Eugenia Price's column.

"Nice fresh style," she commented, as she was counting shoes.

"That's what I thought, but what a shame she's so narrow-minded. I wonder how *she* got mixed up with these people. Think I'll write her a letter."

Gea grabbed the magazine. "Save the letter to write in the

mountains," she exclaimed. "You'll probably get so inspired, no telling *what* you'll say to this writer. Come on, we've got to get packed."

"You taking all this stuff?" I frowned, looking at all the confusion in the room. "I thought we were going to the mountains, you know, the rustic life, goats' milk, coarse brown bread, wooden benches. . . ."

She said haughtily, "Obviously, you have never been to a mountain resort in Switzerland. Well, I haven't either, but I've read and heard plenty. They live it up in these places, and *we're* not going to miss a thing!"

She emphasized the "we're", so I started lining up my things, too, tennis racquet, golf clubs, etc.

Next I ran to the bank to draw out our last reserve. We did have to buy tickets to and from Champéry, and we wanted to get a few small gifts for the Schaeffer daughters.

31. On the following morning, we taxied to the station. We were surprisingly lively, considering we had scarcely slept an hour that night, packing, talking, thinking about the glamorous week ahead. As the driver helped carry in our last piece of luggage, he said, "Have a wonderful summer."

Gea had told him about our good fortune being invited to the mountains.

"Oh," she said, "we're not staying for the summer, only a week or so."

He laughed, "It is difficult to understand women, but have a pleasant trip."

He tipped his hat and bowed.

After we bought our third-class tickets, several other nice people helped us get our luggage on the train, and within ten minutes from the time we entered the station, we were on the train bound for Aigle.

CHAPTER XXI

The Mountains
Come Closer

When Gea and I saw the baggageman start to load the milk cans on the train, which looked as if it had been borrowed from a Walt Disney cartoon, I jumped to my feet and said, "Hey, we can't sit here and reminisce *all* day. Let's throw on our luggage and get going to the mountains."

It was a good thing we started moving, for in a few minutes the small, red train gave the departure signal. I had to shake myself to come back to earth. Talking about our first few months in Switzerland had detached me from the wonderful present moment and the good time ahead of us.

The Disney train kept in character. It followed not an ordinary route. It chugged through the backyards of the people of Aigle. It slowed down for a gardener pushing a wheelbarrow of manure across the track and gave way to some chickens a bit off course. As we passed a chalet where a lady was hanging out her washing on the balcony covered with wisteria and geraniums, the train tooted. The fragrance of flowers was sweet in the air. Everywhere we looked, we saw roses, climbing roses, tree roses, roses in stately rows around vegetable gardens, and roses in front of the Mercedes-Benz garage. The train went parallel to the highway for a short distance where we passed a group of hostelers on bicycles. Then the red train tiptoed around the Aigle hospital, and soon was weaving in and out of vineyards and orchards. As we began to climb the hill to Ollon, we had a superb view of the Dents du Midi. "We're going to be right up close to those mountains," Gea informed me. She being the authority on Swiss resorts.

The train went reverently by an old church, and then stopped at the Ollon station, where there were so many red geraniums in the windows, you couldn't see inside. The train took on more passengers and laughed its way down the other side of the hill into the Rhone Valley, and on across the valley it wobbled, up and over the bridge crossing the rushing blue-green Rhone River.

All the time, Gea and I were twisting our heads this way and that. Everywhere we looked there was something to delight our eyes, and above and around all, the majesty of the Swiss Alps.

"Why haven't we gone to the mountains before?" Gea asked abruptly.

"I was thinking the same thing. What idiots we've been rushing around in the city, when there's all this!"

"Well, of course," Gea reminded us, "the small item of money might have had something to do with it. Say, tell me more about the Schaeffers, are they . . . ."

She was interrupted by something that attracted her out the window. "There's where I'd like to live!" she exclaimed, pointing to a chalet that stood on a small rise of land with the valley spread around it. "I'm glad to be going to the mountains," she said, "but when I settle down, it won't be any five or ten thousand feet in the air. I'm from Kansas, and we like it when you can look out on all sides."

I said, "I'm from Illinois, but that doesn't prove anything. *My* chalet is going to be on a rather small mountain with maybe a sloping field of wild flowers in front of it, like the calendar pictures, and a lovely woods beyond that, and far beyond that, a grand sweep of mountains!"

I made a big gesture to go with my extravagant speech and knocked down a cane that was hanging from the rack above us. The Alpine air had intoxicated us. A weathered old man, who had gotten on at Ollon, sat facing us. He had his rucksack and a bouquet of roses on the seat beside him. As he watched our mounting excitement, he smiled and said in French, "It is the young ladies' first time in Switzerland, n'est-ce pas?" And in a sense he was right.

In a few minutes we arrived at the foot-of-the-mountain village, Monthey. Here we had to change trains again. The weathered old man helped us with our luggage. This time we boarded a real mountain train, one with a cable for the steepest part of the climb. We chose to sit in the last car which was open, without windows; and you could get the best view. We started climbing right away. It was best not to look down. The down was awfully far down, but we looked up and out, and as we went higher and higher, the scenery became more splendid.

We passed close to a few chalets, and we could see children playing on the balconies, a man with a hand plow working a narrow, steep, rocky strip of land, and two women carrying a heavy bucket of water to several white goats dancing about near a barn. We were fascinated by the wood stacked up against the wall of each chalet with such mathematical precision that one would think that each piece had been cut to measure for exacting clients.

"Looks exactly like our woodpile at camp last summer!" I said to Gea with a laugh. That was one of our jobs at camp, to gather wood for fires in the recreation hall. We'd throw the logs and smaller kindling in a heap on the side porch. The marvelous Swiss and their neatness! But there is more than neatness involved in the beautifully stacked woodpiles. When the snow begins to fall, and if it should be a hard, long winter, that wood stored under the low, sloping eaves can save lives; and even two careless Americans can figure out that the closer and neater you stack your wood, the more you can fit into a given area.

The beauty, uniqueness, and charm of Switzerland is not only mountains. Other countries have mountains, but the Swiss use their mountains. They are lived in and cared for. Then it's the "music box" chalets with red geraniums in the windows, Roman bridges, church spires, little green hills, villages nestled in the valley or fitted into a mountainside. It's forests of dark firs with the lighter green larch trees mixed in, decorations on buildings and fountains, cows with large bells around their necks, and the neatness of it all. The simplicity. The stillness.

Up and up we went, and Gea was right, we were getting closer to the Dents du Midi. She was standing up and suddenly she said, "It must be Champéry, looks like the end of the line."

We were the only passengers left in our coach to get off, and there was no danger for one of us to go astray or get left behind, because the train was spending the night in Champéry too.

CHAPTER XXII

The Tightest Spot
of Our Lives

As Gea and I came down the train steps, a very plain lady and a beautiful child walked toward us.

"I am Marlise," the woman said, smiling, "and this is Debbie Schaeffer, and there being no one else, you must be Gea and Betty." She smiled gently at the little girl and said, "Debbie was wondering how we would recognize you. Sometimes the train is full of tourists, and many of them are American; well, no, perhaps more of them are British."

Gea, the authority on Champéry, gave me a knowing look. I had wondered out loud to her why we were the only ones getting off, if it was such a popular summer resort.

Marlise continued.

"First, I must explain to you, Mr. and Mrs. Schaeffer asked me to come and meet you. They were called down to Montreux for a special meeting and won't be back until tomorrow. Now, come along, we'll fetch your luggage."

They had brought along a small wagon for our suitcases. Debbie's big, brown eyes grew even larger when she saw our pile of luggage.

"Marlise," she said, sort of aside and in French, "we should have brought the large wagon." To us, she said, "Oh, excuse me. I forgot. Daddy said I shouldn't speak French in front of Americans."

"*You* are American, aren't you, Debbie?" Gea asked.

"Oh, yes," she replied laughing. "We're from St. Louis and Philadelphia and China."

Marlise, in the meantime, was eyeing our luggage. Gea and I quickly went into a huddle and decided to leave at the station my bags of books, golf clubs, and tennis racquet and come back later to pick them up. With much laughter and joking, we helped Marlise and Debbie pile the remaining suitcases on the wagon.

We felt relaxed and easy with one another by the time we were ready to take off with the tottering pile of suitcases. Marlise insisted on pulling the wagon, and Debbie said that she would help steady it. Gea and I picked up the remaining stray pieces to carry.

We walked around the small station with flowers in every window, passed a lovely little garden, and out into the main street of Champéry, which we soon learned is the only street. There are steep gravel paths leading off it at intervals, wide enough for a car to venture up or down; but if you were going to have friends meet you in Champéry, it would be sufficient to say, "Meet me on the main street." They'd find you.

Even the main street was a narrow road, but it mattered not a bit. The only traffic we encountered that evening were two ladies on bicycles, a few men with packs on their backs and pipes in their mouths, another older lady in a long black skirt and bright red scarf carrying a large bundle of twigs. Farther up the street we met a boy with a stick directing several fat cows with fat bells and a couple of lively goats. Close to the station we passed a small church. Debbie called out, "That's our church"; and on up the street, about in the center of the village, we walked by a large Catholic church. It was an attractive village, and on either side of the road, the "music box" chalets.

Gea, Marlise and Debbie were talking together. I was walking on ahead, enchanted with everything, and simply without words. This was the Switzerland I had been seeking all my life. I had already turned many exquisite pages in my years in Switzerland, but it was as though the artist was saving the best illustration for last. We passed a comfortable hotel, which was a "grown up" chalet with several stories and balconies and geraniums on every floor. Gea called out to me, "That must be where Angela works."

She was a friend we had made through the course we had taken on the Bible and was a student at the famous school in Lausanne for hotel managers and chefs. Angela was spending the summer in Champéry as an apprentice hotel manager.

We walked on past a small ski shop, a tearoom, a store (like a general store with stationery, dresses, pots and pans, and shoes); and then there was a tiny chalet, which was a shoe and ski repair shop. When we came to a clearing, the market place, we all stopped. Les Dents du Midi was directly above and beyond us. It was sunset, and we witnessed one of the thrills of the Alps. The peaks were on fire. The sun was setting below in the valley, and sending up its last wild splash of color for the day in a reflected glow — the splendid Alpine rouge. Gea and I had never seen anything like it. Debbie finally broke the silence. "See," she said, " 'way down there. That's our chalet."

Then for a change, Debbie and I walked together, and Gea helped Marlise with the wagon. We began speaking of many things, Debbie and I, and we talked as if she were an adult too. She was that sort of child. I asked her if she had grown used to Switzerland; I meant, do you reach a stage when it seems ordinary by its familiarity. She said seriously, "No, I never take it for granted. I love living here and am thankful." Then she added, with a sigh, "It makes me wonder what heaven is going to be like! It says in the Bible we haven't seen anything yet!"

The simple beauty and trust in those few words from this child unlatched a compartment in my mind and brought up a memory of another child, many years ago, who also had an uncomplicated faith. I had been an extravagant believer as a youngster, but it had slipped away as I grew older. I couldn't help but think as we walked along that mountain road, what a marvelous thing to be able to believe as a child.

I stole a glance at the girl walking beside me. She is lovely, I thought, so dainty, yet sturdy. Plenty of Swiss cheese and milk and hikes had given her some ruggedness; and yet, she was such a lady, and only six. She started telling me what it is like going to school in the village. Soon we were laughing about foolish little things.

I looked back at Gea and Marlise. They were talking seriously together. How strikingly different, the two. Gea in her extreme hair-do, careful make-up, attractive red dress and smart accessories. Marlise in a full black skirt and plain white blouse, her hair severely pulled back and gathered in a bun. Debbie and I waited for them to catch up to us, and then we entered into their conversation. Marlise had a soft voice and spoke beautiful English. Her passport was Swiss, but her background and experience included several countries in Europe.

We started down a steep hill, and we all helped with the wagon to hold it back, or to keep the luggage from going on ahead. Soon the path leveled off somewhat, and we were in a field of wild flowers. We crossed a wooden bridge over a fast-flowing stream, and as we approached the Schaeffer chalet, it was getting dark. The darkness descends rapidly in the mountains, once the red glow is over.

The old chalet was large, comfortable-looking, but icy cold inside. Debbie showed us to our room on the second floor, and the four of us carried up the luggage.

"When you are refreshed," she said politely, "come down to the dining room, and we'll have supper. Susan and Priscilla, they're my sisters, are *supposed to* be fixing it."

The way she said, "supposed to," led us to suspect Debbie did not have supreme confidence in her sisters' ability to fix supper. Marlise had already gone down to help out.

"If you need anything," Debbie added, as she handed us towels, "let me know."

"She's amazing," I said to Gea, when our young hostess gently shut the door and went out. Gea flopped on one of the beds, kicked off her shoes and moaned, "I'm dead!"

Neither of us said anything for a moment. It was the uneasy silence in which I could feel the dancer-artist-actress-improver of mankind-musician was building up to something.

"Yes, she is a beautiful child," Gea said quietly. Then the tone of her voice changed, and in a slow, mocking whine, she chanted, "Schatzi, old dear, you have written us into the tightest spot of our lives!"

She let the words smolder in the air for a second, then she spit out, "You and your *letters!*"

This was followed by a few swear words in both French and English, as vivid as anything Daniel used to come up with.

"What do you mean?" I asked in honest bewilderment. "We've been in worse places. Don't forget our first pension. This isn't so bad."

I glanced around the room. It was plainly furnished, and freezing cold, now that the evening had come to the mountains, but . . . .

"I'm not objecting to the room," she snorted; and then again in the same mocking voice, "But, Schatzi . . . ."

"Lay off the 'Schatzi' routine," I snarled. "What are you driving at? Why don't you come right out and say it?"

She sat up in the bed, pulled the down comforter around her, and said in a pained way,

"You really haven't caught on, have you? Do all writers live in this dream world? You're so busy staring at cow bells, quaint chalets, fields of flowers, you can't see anything else, or hear, or think! Your *dear* friends," she added, very sarcastically, "and Madame Dumreicher's *dear* friends, are *missionaries!*"

"Missionaries!" I managed to gasp.

"Missionaries," she said in a voice of doom.

"How do you know?" I asked weakly, while I tried to think back over what Madame Dumreicher had said about this family.

"Marlise told me," Gea said simply. "She's one, too. Now please don't fly into a rage, but I would like to ask you one question." She paused dramatically, "Just one reasonable question."

She spoke to me in a quiet, menacing voice, as if she were addressing a child who had just brought back the wrong change from the grocery store, or speaking to an inmate in a mental institution, "Didn't it ever occur to you to ask Madame Dumreicher why this American family was living in Switzerland. What they were doing here? Who they are?"

She groaned, throwing up her hands, "Why don't you just once in life get the facts, get *all* the facts? You, in your slap-happy way, have ruined a couple of weeks for us. We're in for a dreadful week," she sighed. "I could cry."

She looked at the suitcases in the center of the room. "No point in unpacking," she said, "other than to get out my peasant skirt and blouse. We're not going any place, dearie. You and I are *stuck* — stuck for a week in the mountains, far from the rest of the happy world, with a pack of missionaries!"

Having made this dire prediction, she swept the cover over her head in a manner that clearly indicated she couldn't even *bear* the sight of me, the one who got us into this mess.

I reached into my jacket pocket for a cigarette. When I struck the match, Gea lifted her head from under the comforter. "Please!"

she exclaimed, raising both eyebrows. "You're not going to *smoke?*" We missionaries cannot tolerate nicotine, it . . . ."

"Shut up, idiote! Missionaries or no missionaries, they're taking me as I come."

I must have inhaled wrong and broke out into a chain of half-strangled coughs. The lump under the cover made no comment, but I could tell the way it was wiggling, it was laughing. At me.

It was a blow, a real blow. I kept trying to recall the times I had spoken with Madame Dumreicher about the "wonderful" friends in the mountains "you must be meeting." I had met such delightful people through her, it seemed safe to assume these friends would be stimulating, at least, educated, halfway human, but *missionaries. . . .* Good grief!

Gea interrupted my gloomy thoughts. "You know," she said, far more gently than before (Gea's eruptions are like some mountain storms; they arise quickly, and are over as soon), "Marlise is really nice, an intelligent person, I mean, considering she's a missionary, and all that. Do you know what I am going to do before I leave this chalet?"

Her voice had that I've-got-a-terrific-idea ring. Abruptly she threw off the cover, leaped to her feet, made a pirouette around the room, and said with sheer delight,

"I'm going to cut Marlise's hair before I leave!"

And Gea did, of course. She also told me that night before we went down to supper, that we should look on this experience as a challenge — our being stuck with missionaries for a week or so.

"You didn't do too well with turning off the sailor," she reminded me when I, too, began to warm up to the idea of broadening the outlook of these poor, limited creatures. "But maybe you'll fare better at this altitude," she added. "At least, I assure you, they are going to hear from me what I think about people who won't live in the age they're put in and keep reading from an outdated book!"

"They'll hear from me too," I mumbled from across the icy room, half asleep. The only place you could keep warm was in bed with the four blankets and the puff piled on top of you. Suddenly, I felt very weary. It had been a long day.

"Come on," she said, pulling off the covers. "We better go down for supper. Maybe it will be warmer in the dining room. I hope."

CHAPTER XXIII

What a Performance!

The Schaeffers were missionaries all right. Missionaries of the worst sort. They started all meals with long prayers. They talked about spiritual matters from morning until night, and often, far into the night. Whenever Gea and I mentioned a good musical we had seen in Lausanne, or told about the latest French or Swedish movie, somehow the conversation always worked back to Methuselah, Moses, and Mephibosheth, or Shadrach, Meshach, and Abednego.

After dinner, a book of selected Bible verses, something called *Daily Light,* was passed around the table. Everybody read a few verses. Even Gea and I were obliged to stumble through our allotted portion. This was followed by a Bible study conducted by Mr. Schaeffer, and then some praying, quite often by one of the children.

And as if this were not enough, at the point when most civilized people go into the living room to talk about other people, or take a nap, or play cards, the Schaeffer family gathered around the piano and sang hymns.

What a performance!

That's all we could think, that's all we could say: what a performance!

Gea and I had never seen anything to equal it. And what mystified us even more, they enjoyed it! They entered into all of this with great enthusiasm and cheerfulness. As Gea commented to me, "You'd think that they were singing about a king or something."

All we could think those first few days was: What a performance!

You do understand that this was the daily dinner and supper routine, and, oh yes, afternoon tea. If you wanted to eat, and you get a powerful appetite in the mountains, you had to listen in. Mercifully, breakfast was irregular, because nobody in the chalet seemed to be on the same rising schedule.

Gea and I looked forward to breakfast. There we got a little rest and peace. I do not believe that we would have pulled through those first few days without the quiet of the breakfast hour, which we often stretched into hours.

We were the last ones up in the morning, and Debbie served us breakfast on the large lower balcony: large cups of "café au lait" (strong coffee with rich, hot milk), thick slices of coarse bread, the best-tasting cheese, sometimes hard rolls, and always a variety of homemade jams and jellies. The air was fresh and the sun bright and warm. We never tired of sitting on the balcony looking and listening.

The chalet was tucked into a valley in a field of flowers; and on a mountain ridge directly above us we could see one or two other chalets reposing in a patch of bright green grass. From the gorge far below came the melody of water rushing over rocks and pebbles, and all around us were birds singing, wind in the pines, and a chorus of cow bells.

Debbie usually stayed and talked with us for awhile. She explained that her grandparents on her mother's side were missionaries in China, and that her mother had been brought up in China. Then she told us that it was when they were in St. Louis that her father had decided to take his family to Europe. She couldn't remember exactly why, but it was something about making a survey; and they also taught Bible classes. And since they had moved to Champéry, her father had started to hold regular church services for the English-speaking skiers at the small Protestant church we had passed near the railroad station.

When Debbie took our trays back to the kitchen, Susan or Priscilla usually joined us. Susan was the artist in the family, that is, in a rough-and-tumble way. I think I must have been like Susan when I was growing up. She did everything in an exaggerated and intense way, at the same time, rather slap-happy. When Susan was in charge of flowers for the chalet, she didn't skip to the nearest field and pick a few daisies. Not Susan. She climbed one of the

128

higher mountains, hung over cliffs, and came back, hours later, bruised, exhausted, and elated, her basket spilling over with rare flowers. She was breathless with wonder at the beauty she had seen, the adventure she had had. Susan was around ten. For her, life was for living and she was simply and gloriously doing it.

Priscilla was only a few years older than Susan, but becuase she was a different personality, she seemed much older. She was quieter, but not lacking in sparkle, very attractive and extremely quick and bright, like their mother.

We were helping her cut out some paper animals one morning. "What're they for?" Gea asked.

She explained that she helped her mother teach a Bible class. "But where do the children come from?" I asked. She explained, "There are several boarding schools in Champéry, and all these children speak English. Switzerland is full of these finishing schools where parents from all over the world send their children."

"Some are as young as Debbie," Susan added. "Daddy has told us that there is one thing he prays that he will be able to do, and that is to keep our family together while we are growing up."

"Missionary families often get broken up," Pris said. "The children have to be sent away to school, and they never really experience family life."

Gea and I had quickly observed what a wonderful family spirit the Schaeffers had. They thoroughly enjoyed one another; but not in any way that shuts out others, and they had such good times together over simple pleasures. We remained convinced that they were "off" in their religious conviction and their narrow-minded insistence that the Bible is the final truth of the universe; but we were hopeful that *our* influence on *them* would be rewarding, and that they would come to adopt a broader concept of truth. But there was no denying it, they were delightful people, interesting and interested in many of the same things we were. It surprised us greatly to discover how fond we were of them.

CHAPTER XXIV

A Pair of
Swiss Walking Shoes

Late one night Gea and I were discussing the Schaeffers in the privacy of our room, and from under the big puffs. We had thawed out considerably since our arrival at Chalet Bijou, but the bedroom hadn't. It was like sleeping in a ski cabin on top of a mountain.

"Edith doesn't look like a missionary," Gea commented.

"A little louder please, I have my ear-muffs on."

"I *said*, Mrs. Schaeffer doesn't look like a missionary! She reminds me of the ballerina in the Ballet de Paris, remember?"

She continued in a softer voice (I had removed the ear-muffs and tried placing a hot water bottle on top of my head. I recommend this, that is, if you have two hot water bottles, one for your feet too).

"I love the way her eyes sparkle when she talks."

Gea had had time to observe Mrs. Schaeffer carefully as they talked in the kitchen, with Gea sitting on a high stool at the end of the long table in the center of the room, while Mrs. Schaeffer was making pies, homemade bread and orange rolls.

Gea suddenly switched her remarks to Mr. Schaeffer, "He certainly has enthusiasm, and he knows so much. What were you two talking about last night? I noticed even *you* waving your hands a few times. Were you trying to sell him on your United States of Europe?"

I was trying to read, but I gave up; anyway, my hands were too cold to hold the book.

"No, I wasn't trying to sell him *my* United States of Europe," I said. "Gea, how many times do I have to tell you that's not *my* idea. It happens to be a good idea, I am interested in it, and . . . ."

"Please, please, no lecture tonight, I'm tired — whew! these people never go to bed; all I asked was, what were you and Fran talking about?"

"We were talking about modern art and its message. He was saying that a lot of people today look at a modern painting, and almost immediately say, 'I don't like it,' and there are those who actually spit on some of the works. . . ."

"Oh, I don't believe it!"

"Yes, it's true. Kandinsky, in his early period of experimenting with abstract art, wrote about it himelf, how he used to have to wipe off his paintings every night, because people disliked them so much, they spit on them! Now, what Mr. Schaeffer is saying, and I've never heard it said quite this way, he would feel it acceptable for people not to like much modern art. Most of it is not 'likeable,' in the sense of a beautiful seventeenth century still life, but it's not to be ignored. These artists are saying something. They are painting the real despair and blackness of their own souls, they're. . . ."

"OK, OK," I heard a voice murmur from far under the covers, and then a noisy yawn and silence.

I said rather loudly, hoping to wake her up,

"Obviously, some people aren't interested in learning!"

It didn't disturb her at all. It being 3 A.M., I decided to go to sleep myself.

The next morning while we were having our leisurely breakfast on the balcony, Marlise came to tell us that Angela had telephoned from the hotel. "She wonders if you want to go on an all-day hike tomorrow?"

"I'd love to," I said.

Gea frowned, "Hike?" Then she looked at Marlise, "Did she say 'all-day'?"

"I think it's a great idea; then we can ask Edith if she will invite Angela for dinner," I said. "I'd love for her to hear one of these discussions."

Marlise said, as she started back to the study,

"She said you can call her around noon."

Gea called after her, "Marlise, come here a minute!"

131

Oh, oh, I thought, here we go; poor Marlise doesn't have a chance. Gea never did believe in the slow pitch.

"Sit on the railing!" the beauty authority and improver-of-mankind directed. "I wish to study your profile."

Sure enough, I saw it with my own eyes: in a matter of minutes Gea was combing out Marlise's long, fine hair, talking in a soothing voice, and had the scissors poised for action.

Marlise fairly trembled. It was the first time in her life that anyone had cut her hair. Marlise did not really relax (nor I) until later that afternoon when Gea removed the rollers, spent another half-hour shaping, and finally called us to see the finished product.

The new hair style did something wonderful for Marlise, we all agreed; and when finally she had the courage to peek into a mirror, she cried and laughed at the same time, then ran over and hugged Gea.

Pris, Sue and Debbie could hardly wait for Gea to work on them; and so she spent the rest of the afternoon trimming hair, freely giving advice on how to improve one's appearance, and teaching the girls how to walk. I spent the day writing letters. Edith ran back and forth between the kitchen and the living room to see the exciting changes.

"When do you start on me, Gea?" Edith said, smiling.

"I wouldn't change a thing. You're just right!"

"Thank you, Gea," she said warmly. "You're awfully good for morale."

"What's going on in here?" Fran stepped into the living room, "such squealing and laughing!"

"We're being glamorized," Sue explained. "I bet you didn't know that *I* had hidden beauty!"

He looked at his middle daughter, and smiled,

"You've always been beautiful to me, Susan."

"Really?" she said in honest astonishment.

"Really," he said. "Now, I don't want to interfere, but do you suppose I could find a volunteer to go to the station? I'd like to get these letters on the last train."

I came from behind the stove, "I have some letters to mail too. Gea and I will be glad to volunteer."

A few minutes later we had reached the main road, and Gea had stopped to shake the gravel out of her toeless shoes. "Why couldn't you go by yourself?" she grumbled. "These paths kill me."

"Ah, but I'm going for your sake mostly," I said serenely.

I was enjoying myself immensely, ever since the middle of the afternoon, when the idea hit me. She looked at me with suspicion; but I only smiled, in what I hoped was a maddening way, and nothing more was said until we got in front of the general store.

"Why are we going in here?" she demanded, as I opened the door and yanked her in.

The store owner greeted us, and asked what we wanted.

"The young lady wishes to buy a pair of Swiss walking shoes," I said pleasantly and firmly. Gea threw me a wild look; but having studied her technique at close range for nearly one year, I knew exactly how to handle such a case.

"Sit down," I barked. "Remove your shoes."

She was not as difficult as I anticipated. She had been hobbling along the mountain trails long enough to welcome the opportunity to sit down and take off her shoes. The manager brought her a couple of stout pairs to try on. Due to the fact that Swiss women have broader feet than most Americans, Gea had to settle for a sturdy, thick-soled, clumsy-looking pair of mountain shoes that was one size longer than she normally wore, and about three inches wider. The storekeeper did a fine job of padding the shoes; and, by the time Gea put on two pairs of thick, woolen socks, which we also bought in the general store, she walked out of there as if her feet were upholstered.

Gea learned to love those Swiss walking shoes, in spite of the fact she kept bumping into objects. She never learned to judge distances in them, because it was like walking around in a pair of swimming fins; but they were so comfortable on the steep gravel paths that she never once complained.

CHAPTER XXV

Something Began to Click

After we mailed the letter, we stopped at the hotel to see Angela, and to arrange our hike for the following day.

"How you making out with the missionaries?" she grinned at us. "They're kind of balmy, don't you think? I mean, all that praying and singing and . . . ."

It stabbed us to hear Angela ridiculing them, and Gea rushed to their defense. She said hotly, "They are the nicest family I have ever met in my life, Angela. Maybe I don't agree with them straight down the line, but nobody calls them balmy in *my* presence!"

With that outburst, Gea spun around on her new flat heels, marched away, only to bump into a barrel topped with geraniums which stood by the counter in the hotel lobby.

Angela blushed and stammered, "Oh, Gea, come back here. I happen to like the Schaeffers too, but I do think they go overboard on religion."

"I'm not so sure, Angela," I said quietly. "Whatever it is that they believe, it surely hasn't hurt them. They know more about what's going on in the twentieth century than the three of us put together. And furthermore, the more you think about it, there's not much point in believing something, unless you *really* believe it."

"Yes," Angela said, "I don't doubt their zeal or sincerity, but their insistence that Christianity is the ultimate truth in the universe happens to be nonsense, passé, and you two know it! There isn't a respectable school in England that doesn't teach that all religions are equally good, and . . . ."

Something began to click in my mind.

"Angela, excuse me," I said, "but for the first time in my life I'm beginning to see how that old refrain belittles God, to keep saying that all religions are basically the same and basically good. Why, that reduces the supreme being to a status lower than a floorwalker in a department store."

No one was more surprised than I to hear me arguing on the side of the Schaeffers. Even Gea was staring at me with an odd look, but I kept going, "For years I have thought it was the open-minded, intelligent thing to say that all religions stem from the same God, but how foolish that makes God! A foreman in a factory has better organization than the popular, vague god-of-all-religions who tells people to believe anything, do anything, and we'll all come out together at the end! Why . . . ."

"Hear, hear!" mocked Angela, "let's get her a soapbox to stand on!"

Fortunately there was no one in the lobby, so we all felt free to speak our minds. I went on talking, since my momentum was up: "If God made us, and I believe He did — I've never had trouble believing there is a God — it does not make sense that He would throw us out into the world and not bother to communicate with us in a . . ."

We couldn't talk any longer as Angela was on duty, and a group of hikers came in requiring attention. But before we left we arranged to meet at the bridge around eight the next morning; and we also told Angela that Mrs. Schaeffer would love for her to stay in the evening and have dinner with us after the hike.

We did meet Angela the following day, and we had our long walk. Edith had packed a lunch of hard-boiled eggs, pickles, severals kinds of cheese and sausages, hard rolls, fruit, cookies, choco-late, and a thermos of tea. It was a sunny, clear day, and the trail Fran had marked for us was not too steep and part of the time ran through a beautiful forest. Everything was right for an enjoyable outing; but one thing was missing: there wasn't a good spirit among us. Obviously Angela had not appreciated Gea's snapping at her yesterday and my contradicting her. Then for some reason both Gea and I were out of sorts. The night before, we had had a long, strenuous talk with the Schaeffers, and then had re-hashed it in our room until the early hours of the morning.

Several times we tried to talk of amusing things, or comment on the beauty around us, but soon we'd lapse back into an uncomfort-able silence.

As we were coming back down the trail, for a short distance we had to walk along a narrow ridge with a sheer drop-off of a few thousand feet. As we were inching our way along, I thought how close life is to death. Here it was obvious. A careless step, a moment of panic, and all three of us could hurtle into the abyss; but much of life was equally perilous — it's just that we don't see it. Then I began having a maddening experience with a Bible verse that kept playing in my mind like a record that gets stuck. I desperately tried turning it off, but over and over I heard, "For the preaching of the cross is to them that perish foolishness; but unto us which are saved it is the power of God. . . . For the preaching of the cross is to them that perish foolishness; but unto us which are saved it is the power of God. . . . For the preaching of the cross . . ."

What a relief when we passed safely over the ridge and were back on the forest path with level ground and trees on both sides of us. Gea stopped and leaned against one of the tall sturdy pines, "Whew! I'm glad I don't have to walk on that ridge again. One false step there and . . ."

"I was thinking the same thing," I said, "how often we are a step away from . . ."

"You two morbid characters!" Angela cut off both of us. "For heaven's sake," she exploded with a brittle laugh, "let's change the subject!"

We were only too glad to, and soon the three of us were laughing about a friend of ours in Lausanne, who also attended the "hotel" school with Angela, or I should say, he had. Martin, upon opening his first bottle of champagne during his apprenticeship in a restaurant near Lausanne, had trouble getting off the stopper; and when it abruptly shot off, the bottle, unfortunately, was aimed at a neighboring table, spraying a fine mist of champagne upon the guests. Later in the same evening, when he was serving the dessert, one of the ladies at his table suddenly raised her arm as he was lowering a try of cream puffs, raspberry tarts, and chocolate eclairs, and instead of getting the cream puff she had requested, she got a lapful. The evening did help to shape Martin's future life, though. Later he married the cream puff lady, and soon after became the head of a large insurance business she owned.

And that reminded me of Madame Dumreicher and the cat on

the table. Gea had heard the story several times, but urged me to tell Angela anyway. Toward the end of our hike, we had fairly well recovered our usual high spirits; but, as we crossed the bridge near Chalet Bijou, I happened to glance up and my eye fell upon the ridge we had inched across, and the thought of death filled my mind; and I finished off the three of us by asking, "Why do we live if it's only to die?"

CHAPTER XXVI

Infinite Imagination

W hen we entered the chalet that night, we were not only tired physically, but in every way. The Schaeffers, during our stay with them, had exposed us to large doses of Paul's letter to the Romans. Portions of it were hammering at me by forcing my compartmentalized mind to think about death, not to gloss it over as if it was not a reality; and the forceful words were chipping away at Gea by creating a great longing for forgiveness and peace with God.

The girls showed Angela where she could clean up for dinner, and Gea and I went up to our room. We didn't exchange a word. Each one of us was lost in her own thoughts. I am sure the room was very chilly, but for once we didn't comment on it.

As we walked into the dining room a few minutes later, Fran and Marlise were just coming out of the study, each carrying a stack of letters and papers. Fran's tired face lighted up when he saw us, and he said, "We've missed you two today."

Then Angela came into the room, and she was given a cordial welcome. Susan was scurrying around arranging flowers, place cards, and surprises. Debbie was singing as she lighted the candles on the table. Every meal in the chalet had an air of festivity, but this one even more so.

Finally Edith told Priscilla to ring the dinner bell, because by this time both Susan and her father had disappeared. Soon Fran came in the side door with both wood and coal to keep the fire going throughout the evening, and Susan rushed in from the balcony with one last bouquet of roses for the buffet. We all stood at our places, and just before Fran prayed, Edith whispered, "Do you suppose you could shorten your prayer a little? I have some biscuits in the oven. Gea told me last night that she hadn't had baking powder biscuits since she left Kansas."

He smiled gently and said, "Let us bow our heads."

That night during his prayer, instead of looking around and concentrating on a dozen other things, I bowed my head and listened. I couldn't get over it. He wasn't saying a few trite words about "God bless this food"; no, he was sincerely asking his heavenly Father that Gea, Angela, and I might also partake of the everlasting Bread of Life and come to love and trust the Lord of lords and King of kings.

When Gea saw Edith come in with the basket of hot biscuits, she said with a sniff or two, "I'm not crying because I'm sad, but it's just so nice and peaceful here. All my life I've wanted peace inside, but most of the people I know are less peaceful than I am."

Her remark plunged us immediately in a discussion of why so few in our generation have peace of mind. It was either Pris or Sue who said, "To have peace you have to believe God, and few people do today."

One of the others added, "God gives us the power to choose, and the majority of people in this age have chosen not to believe God's Word. One has to base one's life upon the belief that there is ultimate truth in life if one is to have peace, because otherwise we are saying that life is chaotic, and God is not in control."

Angela said, "Yes, but then you are implying that Christianity is the ultimate truth." A bit harshly, she added, "You can never make me believe that!"

Very kindly, Fran said, "You are absolutely right, Angela. Only the Spirit of God can open our eyes to truth. When I was eighteen, I became completely disillusioned about religion, and I was ready to discard the whole business; but before I threw out the Bible, I decided that the honest thing was to at least read it." He laughed pleasantly, "It was a marvelous experience. While reading it I found the answers to my doubts and questions. I became so excited. I thought that I had discovered something new. Certainly it was completely different from what the church I was going to was teaching about Christianity. Actually what I found was historic Christianity, not the synthetic version popular today."

I decided to jump into the conversation too.

"What you're saying, and what you've been telling us all week has jolted me, I'll admit," I said. "I'm like Angela, however — no one can make me believe anything. But you *have convinced* me that I have rejected the Bible, or rather, the authenticity of the Bible, on the flimsiest evidence possible. I'll admit that I have been repeating what I've heard a lot of other people say, that 'the Bible is full of errors and myths.' It does seem quite foolish to throw away something that you haven't bothered to look into yourself."

I started talking faster.

"You know that seminary you were telling me about, the one in Philadelphia," I said to Fran. "Well, first I'm going to spend the whole summer reading the Bible. Then, next fall, I'm going to that seminary, that is, if they'll accept me." With mounting enthusiasm I babbled on, "I'm going to dig this thing out for myself! Steep myself in Hebrew and Greek, read the ancient manuscripts, pour over ecclesiastical history, make a comparative study of the major religions of the world; and then I'll decide for myself if Christianity is what you say it is!"

There was a moment of silence, and then Fran said slowly, "Yes, all that is a good idea, but there is one difficulty. Do you remember what you told me the other night? That you *had,* on a couple of occasions, attempted to study the Bible, but it made little sense to you, and it was dull, you said."

"Yeah," I said, pushing up my glasses and scratching my head.

"Well," he said, "there's a real reason. To understand the Word of God you need spiritual insight, the power of the Holy Spirit to guide you and give you insight. You . . ."

Gea broke in,

"That's all very interesting, but what about my peace? I don't want to go to any old seminary and read thick books, I just want peace deep inside me!"

Edith said, smiling, "You surely don't have to study Hebrew and Greek to have peace, Gea. Thank God it isn't that complicated. We're back to choice. My dear, if you choose even this day to believe in Christ, He will give you peace, and . . ."

Gea began to cry. Her lovely dark hair fell over her face as she buried it in her hands.

"But I don't want to be an old missionary with a bun on the back of my head!" she wailed.

We all laughed at her sudden outburst, and Gea, the hardest, when she realized how funny it sounded.

Edith went and put her arm around her shoulders and said gently, "No one is asking or telling you to be a missionary, Gea! In the first place, no one is going to *make* you accept the Lord. God gives everyone of us the power to choose whether or not we believe in Him. And secondly only the Lord Himself can tell *you* what He has planned for *your* life if you do accept Him as Saviour. Gea," she said, with her eyes sparkling, "we are talking about the infinite God who has infinite imagination! Of this I am sure, if you do accept Him and trust Him, He will make something of your life far better than anything you can work out without Him, and His plan for you will be right for *you*."

Much more was said that evening. We were all pretty strong talkers, little Debbie included. Finally, when we walked Angela back to the hotel, it was way past midnight.

She said, "You're leaving tomorrow, eh?"

"Yes," Gea said. "Call us when you get back to Lausanne, Angela."

"Please do," I added. "After our trip to Sweden in July, we'll be back at the same place, making the same rounds."

She gave us a quizzical look.

"I don't think so," she said pointedly, "but I will call."

CHAPTER XXVII

Unfathomable Love

Our suitcases were packed and down in the hallway. Gea had gone out on the balcony with Susan, who had something she wanted to show her. I had gone up to our room to be sure we hadn't left anything. I was pondering something Mrs. Schaeffer had said to me earlier in the week, and it lodged in my mind. We were talking about faith.

She said, "If I told you I was born in China, you'd believe me, wouldn't you?"

"Yes," I admitted that I would.

"But why believe me?" she asked.

"Well, I suppose it's because I trust you. Even though I haven't known you long, it's registered with me that I can trust you."

"All right, then, using the same logic, if you feel you can trust me with my faults and limitations, then how much more should you trust the men and the method God chose to reveal Himself to us. When you dismiss the Bible with a shrug of your shoulders, you are not only showing your ignorance concerning what some of the most brilliant minds in history have said about the Bible, but far worse, you are calling God a liar."

Suddenly, I had an overwhelming desire to say one last word to Mrs. Schaeffer. I found her in one of the bedrooms changing sheets.

"Edith," I said in a very quiet, matter-of-fact voice, "I've been considering some of the things you've said this week. You know, last night I said I was going to read the Bible this summer and then go to the seminary this fall; and after all that, decide whether I think this is truth or not you're talking about. Well, I have just come to a conclusion. You have said that when someone accepts

Christ as his Saviour, at that very moment the Holy Spirit comes to dwell in him. Well, it seems to me very silly to begin this strenuous program without all the help I can get . . . yeah," I said, and again, "yeah, I think I'll accept Christ right now, and then have that help all through this summer."

Edith Schaeffer, who was pulling a pillow case off its pillow with her teeth, could hardly believe her ears. She had never heard a confession of faith quite like it; but, as she said, God has infinite imagination, and He never turns out two models alike. She dropped the pillow, rushed over and hugged me. Then together we prayed. Gently she suggested that I thank the Lord for dying for me. It felt good to say it, because suddenly I knew it was true.

While we were talking and praying upstairs, Gea stopped a moment in the living room to write something in the guest book. Soon we heard voices calling us, telling us to run, or we'd miss the train; so off we rushed, with Marlise waving from the kitchen door, and Edith calling after us from an upper balcony, "Be sure to keep in touch with us! We'll be praying for you. Good-bye! Good-bye! The Lord bless you."

Priscilla came with us. Fran, Sue, and Debbie had gone ahead with our mound of luggage.

Edith and Marlise could scarcely wait until the others in the family came back from the village to tell them about my last-minute decision. And then as "the pack of missionaries" were rejoicing at what God had done, one of them thought to look into the guest book, and their joy was made richer and fuller upon reading Gea's words:

"Little did I know, that in coming to Chalet Bijou, I would finally find The Christ I've been looking for, for so many years. My gratitude to you for showing me the way."

It has amazed us ever since. There in the Swiss Alps, Gea scribbled her confession of faith in a little book, and I barely nodded my proud head to the King of kings in an upper bedroom because I wanted more understanding; but in His unfathomable love, The Saviour and only Wise God welcomed us into His everlasting kingdom, even us, two fun-loving, ridiculous creatures who seemed hardly at all religiously inclined.

The love I now have for my Lord, the respect, awe, and reverence for God which is growing in me, the reality of the Spirit teaching and guiding me, the knowledge of how much I needed and continue to need God's releasing forgiveness for my sins, all came later. Even for weeks after we were converted, I continued to thank God for forgiving Gea and *her* sins. One day I caught her looking crookedly at me after our prayer time and my usual prayer about *her* sins. I thought sin was all the obvious wrong things you can see; but when gradually it was revealed to me that *that* is only half of the story, and that sin is a much deeper, more complicated thing, and involves our attitude, our disposition of heart, our careless indifference before the holy and just God, then I understood in the depth of my heart, Isaiah's cry, "Woe is me! for I am undone; because I am a man of unclean lips." It takes some of us longer to see ourselves as sinners, but when once we do, we never quite get over the graciousness of God, and the wonder of forgiveness.

The Lord does not draw us to Himself in a fixed, tiresome pattern. Not at all. He is ever mindful that we walk in different shoes, along different paths.

Later in the summer, Gea and I went to England to visit Madame Dumreicher. It was sort of on our way to Sweden. After we had laughed and cried together and shared every wild detail of our visit with the Schaeffer family, and later, while we were having tea, I suddenly thought to ask my old friend,

"Why didn't you *tell* me they were missionaries?"

She placed her ear trumpet in her lap and smiled innocently as she winked at Gea, "Oh, *didn't* I?"

CHAPTER XXVIII

Two Chalets

Around the time I went to the seminary in Philadelphia, Gea went with her husband to South America. Wayne and Gea had known each other for years, but with Gea heading for either the stage or Hollywood, and Wayne for the ministry, it did not seem likely they'd ever get together.

It happened that Gea's mother ran into Wayne downtown in Hutchinson one of the first days after Gea came home from Switzerland. He inquired about Gea, as was his policy over the years, and when he learned that she had had some sort of religious experience in the Swiss Alps, he thanked Gea's mother fervently, and he rushed to the nearest telephone to tell the new convert that he was coming right over. And he kept coming until Gea knew with the same certainty he knew that they were meant for each other, and that this was God's special plan for her life.

Now they are back from South America where Wayne studied in a Lutheran seminary for two years, and he is presently serving as a pastor in a small church near Chicago; and Gea's dream to have a chalet where you can look out on all sides is coming true.

In between teaching school and the other duties in the life of a young minister, Wayne is building his version of a Swiss chalet on a small rise of land in the middle of a field which he purchased from a farmer. The fact that he has never built a barn nor even a bird house does not bother Wayne in the least. The chalet is going up with the help of his father and some members of their congregation and considerable supervising by the minister's wife. Besides having a wonderful, wide balcony and a long basement where the children can play, and Gea and Wayne can save all the antiques they adore collecting, the Illinois chalet is going to have an elevator.

145

Wayne, whose hobby is visiting secondhand stores, auctions, and junkyards, found the friendly little elevator with the brass gate and fixtures in a mansion in Chicago that was being dismantled. He was just about to install the stairs in the chalet when he went to the auction, and he figured that it would be cheaper to install the elevator than the stairs. When you are a poor parson with five children, two dogs, five cats, a turtle, *and* an artistic wife, you have to economize.

And *my* chalet came about this way:

A few years after Gea and I spent our unforgettable week with the "pack of missionaries," I went again to Switzerland. There are certain advantages in doing nothing. While visiting the Schaeffers, who have now moved to another village across the valley from Champéry, I mentioned casually that some day I might buy a little chalet near them and settle down. By "some day" I meant ten or twenty years from now, when I might have saved enough for a down payment.

And so the following year I received a letter from Mrs. Schaeffer. It said, "The last time you were here, you mentioned that some day you would be interested in buying a chalet near us. This letter is only information. We are in no way trying to get your guidance for you, but we feel it only right to tell you that the loveliest chalet we have seen in Switzerland is for sale across the road from us. . . ."

Even before I came to the end of the letter, I could see I had a stuffy notion about "some day." It could mean *right now*. This is one of the many things I like about being a child of the infinite God of infinite imagination. You can be extravagant. And believe me, this is the most reckless, wonderful, wild thing I have done in my life — buying a house I have never seen, with money I do not have, for friends I have yet to meet; and I highly recommend it. God-covered extravagance makes living hilarious, purposeful, and fun.

It is exciting to know your life is fitting into an over-all plan which extends beyond what you can see, do or even imagine. In less than a year after Gea and I cluttered up the Schaeffer chalet, there has scarcely been one weekend that the Schaeffers haven't been overrun with swarms of young people seeking fuller, deeper, richer answers than the ones they are hearing on TV, or in their universities and in many churches.

These students, artists, soldiers on furlough, drug addicts, theologians, musicians, alcoholics, philosophers, dancers, beachcombers, and seekers of truth come with every shade of belief and unbelief possible; and in the place now known as L'Abri Fellowship (which simply means, a place of shelter), they are confronted on all sides with the good news that authentic, historical Christianity can meet their desperate, confused needs too. God is speaking to the twentieth century man as eloquently as He did to Moses, Isaiah, John, Paul, Augustine, Luther, Calvin, and Farel, if we will listen as they did, with their hearts and minds and souls.

Many continue to come to L'Abri along a path similar to the one Gea and I traveled. They arrive hungry, contentious, full of themselves, not knowing Who or what they are seeking; but they knock on the L'Abri door because someone along the way cared enough about them to risk upsetting them in order to set them straight.

CHAPTER XXIX

"Lift That Bale..."

About the time the sixth or seventh mortgage payment for Chalet Chesalet came due, I could see that I would have to get a position with salary. If there were to be "fringe benefits, coffee breaks, picnic and banquet once a year, and pension," fine, but what I needed most was the salary.

For roughly ten years, on and mostly off, I had been working at what I called "writing" and with extraordinary success in creating scarcely a ripple of enthusiasm in the world of editors and publishers. Much writing went out, and much came back. Soon my little beach-house on the edge of Lake Minnetonka, where I had gone to see if I could write if I set my mind to it, became so cluttered with letters of rejection and returned manuscripts that I could hardly find a vacant chair upon which to sit or an open spot on the table to write other manuscripts for editors to mail back.

Enthusiasm and faith I had; all I lacked was knowledge, guidance, technique, wisdom, and discipline; and so exercising the faithful formula — when in doubt, go to school — I enrolled in an evening course in journalism at the University of Minnesota.

Often that winter when I walked across the campus from the parking lot to the Fine Arts Building, the snow crunched and sang under my boots the way it does in below-zero weather, and as much as I hate the cold, I did not miss a session. To me it was fascinating to learn what an art writing is, that there is much more involved than having sharp pencils, piles of clean, white paper, enthusiasm, and a desire to say something. I listened carefully, took many notes and resolved to begin again.

But going to school, attending a couple of writers' conferences, taking a string of correspondence courses, and buying the Swiss chalet ate up most of the trust fund, so when friends in Michigan wrote that they had a wonderful position for me "to help meet the mortgage payments, yet allow *plenty* of time for writing," gleefully I rushed off to Benton Harbor. Lloyd, who was a coach in the junior high school where I was engaged as the librarian, reassured me my first bewildered day at work that this was the ideal job for a writer.

"Why," he said expansively, "there's *nothing* to running the library! Every time I go in there it's nice and quiet and Miss Richards is reading a book or writing a letter . . ."

Maybe if I had stayed twenty-five or thirty years, as Miss Richards had, I too *might* have been on top of the job with time left over to read a book or write a letter, but my entire year in Benton Harbor, the job was on top of me. It nearly flattened me. I didn't even get to the end of September before I had to give up my newspaper column and all other attempts at writing.

Often that autumn, winter, and spring, when I'd finally stagger back to my apartment in the late afternoon and fall heavily on my couch, I would think about Lloyd's remark, that is, on those rare days there was anything left in my mind with which to think. It wasn't that the library itself was so complicated to run, but it had something to do with being shut up in the same building *all day* with 800 healthy, normal junior high school students. It wasn't that they were all bad. Many were wonderful. It was a problem of too much. Too much energy, too much noise, too much everything. And then the one or two difficult personalities on the faculty who had the way of eating up your time, patience, and sanity . . . but that's another story for another book.

Then nothing in my background, nothing, not even the Sea View Hotel on Miami Beach, the summers of biking all over Europe, the Navy, nor twenty-two years of going to school, had prepared me for the Audio-Visual Aid Program. Shortly after I had catalogued and placed a few hundred new books on the shelves, dusted and mended piles of others, plowed into ten or twelve other difficult tasks to familiarize myself with the library, and started to get acquainted with the needs of the students and teachers, I found myself one afternoon with five minutes to myself and nothing pressing that needed to be done. Cheerfully I reached for a piece of paper and a pen to write to Lloyd and his wife, who had now moved to another town, to thank them for getting me this job and that I felt I was beginning to get the library under . . . when the door flew open to my office and the principal (a small, nervous man who *never* seemed overly fond of me nor of anyone) demanded, "Have you checked all the equipment in the visual aid room yet? You *know* the program starts tomorrow, and it's the librarian's job to organize, put in order, and run the projector, show the slides, and arrange with the faculty which students are to see the special films . . ."

I didn't *know* it was the librarian's job to run the projector, etc., and I had *wondered* about all that dusty, broken-down equipment in the room adjoining the library. After the principal scurried away, I walked slowly into the visual aid room and stared at the motion picture projector (with an elaborate, complicated-looking gadget which I assumed was the sound equipment), I wiped a little dust off of a tape recorder, and wondered wildly what to do. I looked with bewilderment at the machines, and they sat there and looked back at me with defiance and hostility.

Sadly shaking my head, I decided to do the direct, honest thing and go and tell the principal that the new librarian couldn't even put a film in a small camera and that she barely knew the difference between a movie projector and a tape recorder, let alone run them.

Talk about upsetting people! ! !

But that was not all that the librarian had to do. About a month before Christmas (it might have been Thanksgiving; all the days seemed alike to me) a high-powered representative from the Curtis Magazine Company came into the library and told me that the principal had sent him up to explain the magazine campaign to the new librarian.

"The *what?*" I asked cautiously.

"The magazine campaign," he repeated heartily. "It's a plan to help young people to learn to be responsible, and I know you'll be just as helpful and cooperative as Miss Richards was in the past few years."

Simply put, it was a plan to sell Curtis magazines, and for the next two months the library was the most slovenly, uproarious, asylum-type place I've ever been in. It involved teams, captains, and sub-captains, and clip boards, reports, and prizes, and thousands and millions of little slippery slips of paper which the sub-captains,

captains and teams got all tangled up and *the librarian* untangled, sorted, classified, made out in triplicate, counted and filed, and then re-counted with the Curtis man who passed by every week or so. . . .

In spite of the fact that during the magazine campaign, I prayed every morning, "O Lord, make me a patient, cheerful, overcoming Christian for just this day," rarely did I even get my foot into the library before I was experiencing the truth of Scripture: "The tongue is a flame of fire. It is full of wickedness and poisons every part of the body" (James 3:6).

It was a grinding, hard year, and many afternoons when I wearily pushed open the door of the junior high school to go home I heard myself humming "Old Man River," particularly the part that goes, "Tote that bar, lift that bale . . ." The rewarding part was making friends with some of the pupils and teachers.

When two of my new friends asked me to go with them to Florida for the spring vacation, I got an idea. It bothered me considerably that many months had gone by and I had not written a word, so I gathered up a manuscript I had been working on before I became the librarian, and rode with my friends to the first small town in the South where I saw flowers and green grass. They helped me get settled in the Jefferson Davis Hotel where I had a living room and bedroom for five dollars a day. There in the warmth, quietness, and friendliness of Murfreesboro, Tennessee, I finished a book which was later published, and it gave me the confidence to give up the salaried position at the end of the school year and go back to writing full time.

So write I did, with flaming determination, for awhile in Chicago, later in a woods near Lake Geneva, Wisconsin. They were lonely years, though wonderful too. Certain things writers and Christians need to know can be learned only in solitude, and although I was not consistently thankful, on the other hand I was thankful to God for my wilderness years. When the time came for me to move to Switzerland to the Lord's little house in the midst of L'Abri Fellowship which the Schaeffers called my chalet and I thought of it as theirs, no one was more surprised than I. I never planned to live in the Swiss Alps, but as Edith Schaeffer often says, "The Lord has infinite imagination. He plans our lives far better than anything we can work out!"

CHAPTER XXX

"A Real, Live Opera Singer"

O ver the years I continued to keep in close touch with the Schaeffers, visited them a couple of times, and on their historic trip back to Switzerland in 1954, a few months before they were put out of Champéry, I went along to keep an eye on their lively, healthy son, Frankie. And in the months immediately following the trip across the Atlantic aboard ship, when he was recovering from polio, in between reading to him, playing games, and drawing pictures, we would carry on this dialogue:

"Did I really run across the ocean?" he'd ask.

"Yes, Frankie, you ran across the ocean," I'd answer. "I *know*, because I chased you across Deck A, up to the Captain's quarters, down to the dining room, over to the shuffleboard deck, up to the poop deck, down to the engine room, into the gym . . ."

And we would go through it all again and again and again . . .

When I returned to the States, I began writing to some of the new Christians Edith told about in her "Family Letter," particularly the more colorful ones. In one letter she wrote about an opera singer who had arrived in Huemoz not knowing what to expect, but she had come for the Easter weekend mostly to get away from the chill and gloom of Milan, Italy. Her story was warm, highly dramatic, amusing, interesting, fantastic, and very real. I looked forward to meeting Jane Stuart Smith one day.

I was like Debby Schaeffer who had never met "a real, live opera singer," and so while I still was the librarian in Benton Harbor, Miss Smith wrote to me from Vienna that she was coming to Chicago for an audition and she wondered, "if Illinois was near Michigan and could we meet?" (Even yesterday when we were planning the L'Abri Ensemble tour for 1970 she was wondering if St. Louis is near Cleveland) . . .

I was thankful Illinois is near Michigan and excited at the thought of having something to look forward to besides the library, visual aid program, and the magazine campaign. And so in a couple of weeks we met. Instead of my learning about opera as I expected to, the singer spent long hours talking about the Lord and how she felt certain He was leading her away from the theater, but she did not have the courage to tell her mother, her maestro, and her manager.

"Opera has been my whole life and it's theirs too," she groaned. "We're all in it together. You don't make a career in the theater on your own. And, furthermore, there is a part of me that loves opera." She sighed deeply, "They'll think I have lost my mind!"

She paced around the room, made extravagant gestures, like an opera singer, I thought, but recalling quickly, this is not the stage. She was struggling with a problem that had deep roots in the past and large possibilities in the future. The time to choose had come.

In real agony she said, "I don't know when I have been in a more tearing situation."

At the time I was what might be called, not-a-clear Christian, and I couldn't see why she couldn't stay in opera. Why make all this fuss and confusion? . . . When I think back to that moment and wonder what would have happened if Jane had listened to me rather than to the living, personal, infinite God, I shudder to think of all those who would have been shut out of heaven if Jane had gone only half the way with the Lord, rather than all the way. As Gladys Hunt has written about the singer, "If you could know the people whose lives have been changed by their contact with Jane Stuart Smith . . . you would understand that her energies are wisely invested."

Not knowing how to help her that day in Chicago, suddenly I thought to say, "Why don't you go and stay in Chalet Chesalet, Jane, until you know for sure what the Lord has for you to do?"

She thanked me in the way a person thanks some one for making a suggestion which is kind but in no way answers the problem.

We talked about many things that weekend. I was astonished at the number of Christian books she had read. She kept asking,

"Have you read McCheyne?" "Have you read John Newton's Letters?" "Have you read the life of Whitefield?" etc., etc. She had a way of firing questions at you, and before you could answer, she was asking enthusiastically, "Don't you think Huss, Luther, and Calvin are great men?" and soon she was talking about favorite painters, composers, sculptors, musicians, theologians, artists, poets, and architects, beginning with the six world powers before Christ.

Also we talked and laughed about the circumstances in which each of us had met the Schaeffers in the Swiss Alps, and how thankful we were to God for their clear witness. When we parted, neither of us had any idea that the next time we would meet, it would be in Switzerland where Jane would already be living in Chalet Chesalet and working at L'Abri. She had several very painful experiences to go through before that time came, however; but the time did come when she left the opera world to devote her whole life to serving God.

When she first started working with the Schaeffers, none of them knew what it would lead to or how long it would last, but they particularly appreciated (and still do) her kind of help. The opera singer was willing to do anything, and if she had never fixed a meal for twenty people or dug manure into the ground to prepare it for a garden or washed heavy Swiss sheets in a bath tub, she was willing to try.

She did not sing for a long time after she became a helper at L'Abri, but she did practice enough to keep her voice in readiness for the time when the Lord would want her to sing again.

Even when I moved my typewriter and books into an upper room in Chalet Chesalet to see if I could write there, she was still singing only to the pots and pans in the kitchen, the heavenly host, and her Swiss neighbor, who listened from his orchard with tears in his eyes as the beautiful full voice sang out across the field.

After Herr Lengacher (The Beeman) became a Christian, he told everyone he met, "It was the singing of Miss Jane which first opened my heart."

To show his thankfulness to his Lord and Saviour and his recognition of the importance of music in a Christian community, he and his brother built a small but beautiful chapel for L'Abri with windows on the side looking out on the Dents du Midi and the Rhone Valley.

CHAPTER XXXI

Like a Symphony

Besides the stirring church services, prayer meetings, and lectures which take place in the chapel, it would be difficult to say how many concerts have been held there in the past few years, and how the former opera singer has stirred up an interest in good music in our community. Only last night at an art and music lecture given in the Chesalet living room a young man from England told the roomful of people that he had spent a few weeks at L'Abri last summer, and for the first time in his life he considered the truth that what you listen to and what you look at profoundly affects what you think and believe.

"The only music I knew well was 'The Rolling Stones' — in fact, I let it batter me," he said. "But when I got back to London after last summer, I checked out every Bach record the British Museum had. For three months I saturated myself in Bach. At first it sounded tinny. Then I sort of began to like it, and then it really got to me." He went on with excitement, "I realized this was real music, and the other stuff is tinny, and the whole rotten life I was living was tinny. I wasn't in the real world at all." He said several other things, and ended his remarks by saying, "Now I know that the real world is the Christian world."

This opened up a wonderful discussion which lasted far into the night. . . .

How Jane sold her opera costumes to give the money for the chapel, how we met Mr. Flentrop who later built us one of his jewel-box organs, how the L'Abri Ensemble was formed, these and many other joyous, thanks-be-to-God stories have been told in other books about L'Abri.

Once in awhile people ask what I do at L'Abri. I answer, really nothing — nothing official, that is, because I am not a member of the work. I just "happen" to live in the midst of it. But as I said toward the beginning of the book — doing nothing can be quite exhausting.

Like one day I was writing in my study when a parade of cows walked by the window. As you probably know about Swiss cows, each one has a handsome bell of varying size and different timbre and pitch. It is one of the most joyous sounds in the world to hear the Swiss cows going up to the higher pastureland in the spring-time. It's like a symphony, I thought, and leaped excitedly to my feet, rushed around to set up the tape recorder and microphone, and if you think it was easy hanging out the window with the mi-crophone in hand, I tell you it was perilous, and just then the singer came out of the woodshed and cried out,

"What are you *doing* hanging out that window?"

We had to do it all over the next day when another troop of cows danced by, because all I got on the first recording was her voice. But on the second trial I let her hang out the window. It turned out better than we dared hope, then because I wasn't doing anything too pressing, she had me listen to twenty or thirty tapes on file to see if we could work the cowbell symphony into a place on a record. After weeks and months of work, we came out with the record, "Joy to the World." The opening selection is the Swiss cowbell symphony.

As I have said, doing nothing is strenuous. For example, one of those Swiss-calendar-picture days a few years ago I was standing on the Chesalet balcony looking down on the spot where the Bee-man had driven stakes to outline the proposed chicken coop. I saw the former opera singer walking about the place very pleased at the thought of getting her chickens out of the dark, crowded wood-shed into a cheerful home of their own. Suddenly I shouted to her, "Over my dead body are those chickens going to have the best view in Switzerland!"

"What?" she said, rather startled to hear a gruff voice coming from the balcony on such a beautiful day.

Loudly I repeated my message, "Over my dead body . . ." etc., etc., etc.

She yelled back, "Would you please come down here and talk sensibly — all I can hear is something about a dead body!"

156

While she dug in some compost around the fruit trees, I sat on the fence and explained my idea.

"That's the perfect place for a guest house," I said with feeling. "I can't stand the thought of wasting that view on *chickens,* why, it's . . ."

She straightened up and said pointedly, "Be careful what you say! You're not talking about just any old chickens. Don't ever forget they helped buy an organ!"

It was true. It is surprising and wonderful what one can do with egg money, particularly when the hens are subsidized by the owners. Vividly I remembered the night at choir when the choir director (Jane) announced that our eggs were for sale at fifty centimes apiece, two for a quarter, that is.

"But that is twice as much as they charge at the village store," complained an alto.

"Yes, but these hens are buying an organ," said the choir director indignantly.

"Great guns! I've heard everything," moaned a tenor, "but never have I heard of a chicken coop with an organ!"

"The organ is for the chapel!" hissed the director.

Not only were the hens subsidized by the owners, but one night we found an envelope on the piano with a check and a note from the donor explaining that she didn't think the hens would resent a little outside help . . .

"Well, it's true," I said mellowing a bit remembering their illustrious history, "they are remarkable chickens, so if you don't mind shoveling your way through the deep snow in the winter to care for them, I give way. They can have this beautiful place to live. Of course," I added gravely, "let's not forget the foxes! The hens will be more vulnerable to attack down here, and . . ."

She looked *very* thoughtful, and said, "A guest house would be nice." Slowly she added, "And I don't think the chickens *really* object to the woodshed . . ."

"And think of how well they lay," I said. "I believe I read in the *World Book* that it upsets a chicken to travel and . . ."

"Yes," she said interrupting me, "a guest house would be wonderful, a place where we could invite musicians to come, and," she added earnestly, "the chickens can help us meet the mortgage payments."

They are doing this, of course.

By the time some relatives of mine arrived from Illinois that summer, the guest house had started to rise (now called Chalet Poulet which in French means chicken house). As my uncle walked around the edifice, he said, "Your chicken house will be standing long after the Faust Hotel is torn down. They are building it to last 500 years!"

That might be true, and again it might not.

It *is* good to know it will stand there as long as the Lord will have it. And it is true about our lives too, and any life that is committed into God's hands. He will do with us what He knows is best for us. What more can a person want out of life?

As it says in Proverbs 3:5, 6: "Trust in the Lord with all thine heart; and lean not unto thine own understanding. In all thy ways acknowledge him, and he shall direct thy paths."

Now I *know* why the sailor was always quoting Bible verses. Why talk about lesser things, when you have discovered the best!

"The Lord says: Let not the wise man bask in his wisdom, nor the mighty man in his might, nor the rich man in his riches. Let them boast in this alone: That they truly know Me, and understand that I am the Lord, loyal, kind and good to everyone, and that I love to be this way to My people" Jeremiah 9:23, 24.

"The grass withers, the flower fades beneath the breath of God. And so it is with fragile man. The grass withers, the flowers fade, but the Word of our God shall stand forever" Isaiah 40:7, 8.

"I know very well how foolish it sounds to those who are lost when they hear that Jesus died to save them. But we who are saved recognize this message as the very power of God" I Corinthians 1:18.